Life Changing

ANSWERS TO DEPRESSION

HAROLD IVAN SMITH

HARVEST HOUSE PUBLISHERS
Eugene, Oregon 97402

LIFE-CHANGING ANSWERS TO DEPRESSION

Copyright © 1985 by Harvest House Publishers
Eugene, Oregon 97402

Library of Congress Catalog Card Number 85-60123
ISBN 0-89081-471-6

Printed in the United States of America.

PREFACE

In a family where tears were not tolerated from boys, an eight-year-old raced excitedly to his grandmother.

"Grandmother!" he shouted. "I've learned to do something that's really super!"

"What have you learned that's so special?" she asked.

The boy beamed. "I learned how to cry inside my brain so that no one can see!" The grandmother gasped at the boy's statement. No longer would he be teased or scolded by his "macho" father for crying. "Isn't that something?" the boy added.

Through the tight lump in her throat the grandmother forced out the words, "Yes, Robert. That is something..."

Tragically, many Christians have learned how to be depressed "in their heads" so that no one can see. Oh, they have heard the cassettes and sermons, read the books and articles. They have memorized the cliche "Christians don't get depressed! We have Jesus!"

But they are still depressed!

Many depressed people have been forced to disguise or hide their depression. Many have pulled into tight cocoons where they can be alone with the blues. They fear that someone will discover their secret, but they long for someone who can understand. Too many have slipped into deeper depression and have been classified "clinically depressed."

Every human being must experience depression. You may choose to use clever synonyms. You may mask or even deny the symptoms. But "the blues" are no respecters of persons. If you breathe, you're eligible.

If you were to ask, "What do you know about depression?" my answer would be, "I know." There are no scars but there are memories. This book is written by a pilgrim rather than an expert. When I read Don Baker's *Depression: Finding Hope and Meaning in Life's Darkest Shadow*, I asked, "What would he know about depression?" until I read this passage:

> I appeared healthy, without bandages and without crutches. There were no visible scars, no bleeding, and yet there was that endless, indefinable pain that no doctor's probing finger could locate—no drug that could totally relieve. There was always the pain and with it the desire for oblivion—an oblivion that would come only in minute snatches of restless sleep.[1]

"Ah, he knows!" I said to myself, and continued to read. *Depression is a reality among believers!* We are not granted immunity through some magic vaccine. The Jews asked, "How shall we sing the Lord's song in a strange land?" God knows that you are trying to sing and make sense of your depression in a strange land.

Sometimes I don't feel like singing praise choruses. Sometimes it has been a major accomplishment just to make it to church. But the same Bible which commands us to make "a joyful noise unto the Lord" encourages us to *"be still* and know that I am God" (Psalm 46:10 KJV).

It is possible to be so busy "making a joyful noise" that we don't hear the wounds of other believers. We need to experience that equally majestic sound of silence: awe. When we stand in God's presence and simply wait. When no word in all the human vocabulary can possibly express our thoughts, our needs, our longings.

Depression has been a part of my pilgrimage. There are some things I've learned on this journey. I'd like to share them with you. If you will take a little time each day to read and think, I believe you will find light at the end of the tunnel. I can't promise you a miracle, but I can promise you that you'll be better equipped to "befriend" your depression—whether a frequent or occasional visitor.

CONTENTS

BECK DEPRESSION INVENTORY

Carefully read through the following statements. Pick out the statement in the group that best describes the way you feel today, right now!

Read all the statements before you make a choice.

1. **_SADNESS_**
_____ I do not feel sad
_____ I feel blue or sad
_____ I am blue or sad all the time
_____ I am so sad or unhappy that it is quite painful
_____ I am so sad or unhappy that I can't stand it

2. **_PESSIMISM_**
_____ I am not particularly pessimistic or discouraged about the future
_____ I feel discouraged about the future
_____ I feel that I have nothing to look forward to
_____ I feel that I won't ever get over my troubles
_____ I feel that the future is hopeless and that things cannot improve

3. **_SENSE OF FAILURE_**
_____ I do not feel like a failure
_____ I feel I have failed more than the average person
_____ I feel I have accomplished very little that is worthwhile
_____ As I look back on my life all I see is failure
_____ I feel I am a complete failure as a person

4. *DISSATISFACTION*

_____ I am not particularly dissatisfied
_____ I feel bored most of the time
_____ I don't enjoy things the way I used to
_____ I don't get satisfaction out of anything anymore
_____ I am dissatisfied with everything

5. *GUILT*

_____ I don't feel particularly guilty
_____ I feel bad or unworthy a good part of the time
_____ I feel quite guilty
_____ I feel bad or unworthy practically all
      the time now
_____ I feel as though I am very bad or worthless

6. *EXPECTATION OF PUNISHMENT*

_____ I don't feel I am being punished
_____ I have a feeling that something bad may happen
      to me
_____ I feel I am being punished or will be punished
_____ I feel I deserve to be punished
_____ I want to be punished

7. *SELF-DISLIKE*

_____ I don't feel disappointed in myself
_____ I am disappointed in myself
_____ I don't dislike myself
_____ I am disgusted with myself
_____ I hate myself

8. *SELF-ACCUSATIONS*

_____ I don't feel I am any worse than anybody else
_____ I am critical of myself for my weaknesses
      and mistakes
_____ I blame myself for my faults
_____ I blame myself for everything bad that happens

9. **SUICIDAL IDEAS**

_____ I don't have any thoughts of harming myself
_____ I have thoughts of harming myself but I wouldn't
follow through
_____ I feel I would be better off dead
_____ I feel my family would be better of if I
were dead
_____ I have definite plans about committing suicide
_____ I would kill myself if I could

10. **CRYING**

_____ I don't cry any more than usual
_____ I cry more now that I used to
_____ I cry all the time now—I can't stop
_____ I used to be able to cry but now I can't

11. **IRRITABILITY**

_____ I am no more irritated now than I ever am
_____ I get annoyed or irritated more easily than
I used to
_____ I feel irritated all the time
_____ I don't get irritated at all at things that used to
irritate me

12. **SOCIAL WITHDRAWAL**

_____ I have not lost interest in other people
_____ I am less interested in other people than I used
to be
_____ I have lost most of my interest in other people
and have little feeling for them
_____ I have lost all my interest in other people

13. **BODY-IMAGE CHANGE**

____ I don't feel I look any worse than I used to
____ I am worried that I am looking old or
       unattractive
____ I feel that there are permanent changes in my
       appetite and they make me unattractive
____ I feel that I am ugly or repulsive-looking

14. **WORK RETARDATION**

____ I can work about as well as before
____ It takes extra effort to get started at doing
       something
____ I don't work as well as I used to
____ I have to push myself very hard to do anything
____ I can't do my work at all

15. **INSOMNIA**

____ I can sleep as well as usual
____ I wake up more tired in the morning than
       I used to
____ I wake up 1-2 hours earlier than usual and find
       it hard to get back to sleep
____ I wake up early every day and can't get more
       than 5 hours of sleep

16. **FATIGUE**

____ I don't get any more tired than usual
____ I get tired more easily than I used to
____ I get tired from doing anything
____ I get too tired to do anything

17. **ANOREXIA**

____ My appetite is no worse than usual
____ My appetite is not as good as it used to be
____ My appetite is much worse now
____ I have no appetite at all anymore

18. **WEIGHT LOSS**

____ I haven't lost much weight, if any, lately
____ I have lost more than 5 pounds
____ I have lost more than 10 pounds
____ I have lost more than 20 pounds

19. **HEALTH**

____ I am no more concerned about my health than usual
____ I am concerned about aches and pains or upset stomach or constipation
____ I am so concerned with how I feel or what I feel that it's hard to think of much else
____ I am completely absorbed in what I feel

20. **INDECISIVENESS**

____ I make decisions about as well as ever
____ I try to put off making decisions
____ I have great difficulty making decisions
____ I can't make any decisions anymore

21. **SEX DRIVE**

____ I have not noticed any recent change in interest in sex
____ I am less interested in sex than I used to be
____ I am much less interested in sex now
____ I have lost interest in sex completely

The Beck Inventory is used with the permission of the Center for Cognitive Therapy, Philadelphia, Pennsylvania, Aaron Beck, M.D., Director.

In love He made us,
In love He will mend us!
                    —Frederick Beuchner

****

Depression is an emotion that can be used
rather than wasted!
                    —Elizabeth Skoglund

****

How precious it is, Lord, to realize that you are
thinking about me constantly!
                    —Psalm 139:17 TLB

GOAL 1 ❖ ADMITTING YOUR DEPRESSION

Depression Is Growing

It was a typical Sunday paper. As I read through the first section, in four unrelated articles I found the words *depression* or *depressed*.

Four times in one section of the Sunday paper? Depression must be getting worse. "Yes," admit psychologists, who have termed this "the Age of Depression." The National Institute of Mental Health estimates that 8 million people are treated annually for depression. Of these, 250,000 will require hospitalization.[2]

More stunning, however, is the NIMH's suggestion that perhaps 30 million people suffer from *untreated* depression. *Thirty million!*

Americans love numbers, statistics, and graphs. Rollo May said that Americans don't believe that a "thing or experience is real until we have made it mathematical." In other words, "What are my chances in getting it?"[3]

Admittedly statistics are used to gain research funds, and therefore the bigger the numbers the bigger the bucks. And admittedly the media make much of the higher numbers. If a report says that between 10 and 20 million people are depressed, on the 6 o'clock news that it will be the 20-million figure that's reported.

However, one reason why depression appears to be growing is that the term "depression" is clinically understood.

15

Earlier in the century the mood was called "melancholia." But that didn't describe the experiences of many people, so they didn't think of themselves as melancholic.

Moreover, talk shows and popular magazines have given celebrities the opportunity to share their personal lives and tragedies. Many stars have admitted their depression, and Americans love to identify with their heroes. Further, the stigma has been reduced as more families have been affected.

Depression certainly is not new. It has always been part of mankind's repertoire of emotions. Adam and Eve discovered depression as well as indigestion after their disobedience.

Today we have a term: *depression*. But think of the millions of people who have died too ashamed or afraid to admit their depression! How many have wrestled their moods in silent despair?

I question if depression is significantly growing. The computer has given us a way to keep better statistics. But the statistics can bring comfort. You are not some strange breed because you are depressed. You are a human being touched by the blues.

There will be a tomorrow untouched by depression. I cannot tell you when tomorrow begins, but it will come. And it will come more quickly if you make some choices. But first let's turn our attention to the sounds of depression.

The Sounds of Depression: "I'm Not Hungry"

Loss of appetite is a common complaint among the depressed. According to folklore, the way to a man's heart is through his stomach. When people have gone to great trouble to prepare a favorite dish, they are hardly amused by your response, "I'm not hungry!"

John's wife says, "I always know when he's depressed. He won't eat, no matter what I make." Beck's study of severely depressed individuals found that three-fourths of them reported some loss of appetite. Beck offered three levels of change in appetite:

Mild: The patient no longer eats his meals with the customary degree of relish or enjoyment. There is some dulling of his desire for food.

Moderate: The desire for food may be gone and the patient may miss a meal (or two) without realizing it.

Severe: The patient may have to force himself (or be forced) to eat. There may be an aversion to food. After several weeks of severe dieting, the amount of weight loss may be severe and dangerous.[4]

For example, Mary is recently widowed and struggles with depression. She can't eat because of the memories and she doesn't want to cook for just one person. So she skips meals. That in turn leads to even deeper bouts with depression. Mary is now learning to *force* herself to eat and cook. Her counselor suggested that she invite a few friends for sandwiches and dessert. Mary agreed to try. She found it such a pleasant experience that she is now planning to invite friends for a full meal.

One widow in Dallas fought mealtime depression for months until she decided to put her gift of hospitality to work. She asked her pastor and his wife to invite six new members or recent church visitors to her home for dinner. After a year, the program has been a smashing success. It gives her a chance to use her china, crystal, and linen. And she now knows more new members than anyone in her church and gets more invitations to dinner. Now depression is rare. Also, she generally has plenty of leftovers for good nutritious meals for one person.

Mealtime depression can also be a problem for those who travel in their work. Judy, a young management trainee for a Fortune 500 company, hates to eat alone, particularly in hotel restaurants or coffee shops. Often she either goes without or calls room service. After three years on the road, all the menus sound alike. "Then I end up thinking about my sister and her family in their big old country kitchen. Then I get depressed." (Meanwhile, her sister fantasizes about all the expense-account meals in exciting restaurants!)

The Jews go one step further: They realize that some people must be forced to eat—not necessarily intravenously, although that too can become necessary. Like Protestants, after a death they bring food to the home. However, the Jews may actually take a spoon or fork and feed the person. It's accepted because it is tradition. Someday the places will be switched: The one who feeds will be fed.

Perhaps that is why Jesus chose to have a last meal with His disciples, even though the Last Supper must have been difficult for Him. He knew that in the hours ahead his disciples wouldn't feel like eating. So he disciplined His own pain and said, "Eat!" How fitting that the living commemoration of His death was a meal!

Finally, poor nutrition is a factor in depression. Many

pleasant family meals have become battlegrounds, with arguments leading to postmeal depression (and probably indigestion).

Do yourself a favor: "Eat!"

It is not so much what happens to you—but how you choose to respond!

The Sounds of Depression: "No One Understands"

One of the subtle temptations in depression is the recurring thought, "No one understands what *I* (and the *I* is always in neon) am going through!" This is especially true for men who cannot admit their depression. Since they cannot exchange symptoms or feelings with other men, they struggle alone.

Abraham Lincoln struggled with depression throughout most of his life. Fortunately, he had a friend, Joshua Speed, who "understood." Speed once remarked, "I never saw so gloomy and melancholy a face in my life."[5] Yet Speed took a liking to Lincoln and became a spiritual brother to him. As bachelors, they swapped jokes and confessed their mutual difficulties in courting. Speed became Lincoln's confidant.

Years later, when Lincoln broke an engagement with Mary Todd, he needed someone to listen to him. But by this time Speed had sold his store and had moved back to Kentucky. . These events threw Lincoln into a deep depression. For one week in January, 1841, Lincoln lay in his room in absolute despair. He cried out, "I am now the most miserable man living. If what I feel were equally distributed to the whole human family, there would not be one cheerful face on earth." Was Lincoln exaggerating? Hardly. He moaned, "To remain as I am is impossible. I must die or get better!"

Then Lincoln visited Speed, and that reunion helped him shake his depression. Eventually he proposed to and married Mary. Yet Lincoln remained a moody, depressed man, given to long introspections about death and illness.

There would have been no great President Lincoln if there

had not been a friend who understood what the future president was experiencing.

Joshua Speed illustrates the power of lay helpers. He had never had a psychology course or read any self-help psychology books. He simply opened his ears and his heart to Lincoln.

It is too easy to think that our problems and burdens are so unique that no one else could possibly understand them. Whatever we experience—*whatever*—someone understands.

Researchers have found that depressed individuals enter new relationships with three burdens:

- *Feelings of helplessness:* "No one can help *me!*"
- *Vulnerability:* "What if they talk about *me?*"
- *Low self-esteem:* "Who would want to help *me?*"[6]

Sometimes our first words turn off the potential helper. It is possible to be so focused on our own depression that we overlook the needs of other people.

Jesus was interrupted on His way to the cross. Peter had angrily cut off the ear of one of the Roman soldiers. Yet Jesus healed the man on the spot. Jesus had to interrupt His own pain and distress to reach out to another person. Sometimes you will have to do the same.

The Sounds of Depression: "Nothing I Try Works Out"

Things are seldom as bad as they seem. Yet a depressed person may have a failure list. "I tried and failed, so therefore—

- I'm not going to try that again!"
- I'd better not risk it!"

Someone wrote, "the best-made plans of mice and men often go astray." And you've invested so much in some of your plans that failure invites depression.

Rich is depressed and repeatedly says, "*Nothing* I try *ever* works out." He applied to medical school and was rejected. So he worked for a biological supply house. Then he taught high school biology and chemistry. Then he worked for his father-in-law selling insurance. Then he—the list goes on. His resume is long, but short on success.

In fact, for six months he didn't work at all. He was paralyzed by his fear of a job interview. Afraid that his next prospect would turn out to be just another line on the resume. Meanwhile his wife wearied of trying to defend him against her father's charge, "You should never have married him!" She was also wearied by trying to make ends meet and has grown disenchanted with their relationship.

Rich still has his fantasies. If only he had gotten into medical school, everything would be different. He would have status, money, a nice car—*if only.* In essence, Rich has never put to rest that first failure. He has sabotaged himself on every subsequent job.

Maybe Rich sounds a lot like you. Unrealistic expectations taunt a lot of depressed people. Have you honestly assessed your lost opportunities?

This kind of self-analysis is painful. It's easier to just stay depressed—much easier.

Let me ask you a question: Have you *never* been successful at *anything* you tried? Have you failed at *everything*? If yes, then you have a right to be depressed. But if you have tasted one success, however small, no matter how long ago, you're statement is not accurate.

No wonder you're depressed! Your brain argues, "What about the time you—" but you keep saying, "Sshh!"

- Did you ever plant seeds and eat the vegetable or smell the flower?
- Did you ever plant a potato and eat it as French fries?
- Did you ever plant a flower and later make a bouquet?

Take a few moments and list the things you've achieved.

- I've _____.
- I've _____.
- I've _____.
- I've _____.
- I've _____.

See? You've been fibbing to yourself, *deliberately* overlooking some of your own achievements. Well, no more of that!

Some famous achievers have uttered your words, "Nothing I ever try . . ." but a generation later, even a century later—

- their poems are still being memorized.
- their songs are still being sung.
- their buildings are still standing.
- their inventions are still valued.
- their trees are still giving shade.

Sometimes only *time* will invalidate your negative statement. So don't be depressed. The jury's still out.

Remember this: Often the reason we are depressed with the results of our labors is that we are rating our achievements by the wrong standards.

Start telling yourself the truth. You'll be surprised at what this will do to your depression.

> **If we were better acquainted with those who have been severely depressed, we might be easier on ourselves.**

The Sounds of Depression: "What Friends?"

It's easy for a depressed person to believe that his friends are abandoning him or talking about him.

But friendship is a two-way street. To have friends you've got to plant "friend seeds." Have you put your eggs in too few baskets, so that when you need a friend none is available? "But I need a friend *now!*" whines Sheila. Friendships are like money in a bank account: To take out you must have previously deposited. Sheila doubts her friends' sensitivity.

"They're talking about me—behind my back!" Sheila scowls.

"How do you know?"

"I can tell!" she snaps.

Admittedly, some of her friends may be talking about her, though not necessarily gossiping. Your depression is to some of your friends like a jigsaw puzzle: Some of the pieces are missing. So they exchange impressions, express their concern, and discuss how they can jointly help you. Sometimes through such conversations someone gives them an idea of something they can do to help you.

The next time you're tempted to conclude that your friends are abandoning you, give it a second thought. Is that *really* true, or are you using self-pity self-talk? Are you bearing false witness against your friends?

"No one cares!" is dramatic. But is the statement *really* true? Why did Christ suffer and die if "no one cares"? His death invalidates your statement, for if just one person cares, your words aren't accurate.

Admittedly, not everyone will respond *as you wish*. Not everyone will drop everything and come running to help you. But it is possible to become so wrapped up in your own pain that you don't hear the pain of other people. Experiments in the area of peer comfort have had surprising results.

In one hospital a severely depressed woman was placed in a ward with ten other patients. Because of financial cutbacks, there was inadequate staff for the patients. So this lady began reaching out to others: carrying food trays, brushing hair, comforting. Her actions produced a change in that ward. In a short time she impacted the lives of many people and recovered from her own depression.

Ironically our "nobody cares" attitude may keep people at a distance. They are afraid to invade your territory. Your "nobody cares" sounds to them like "Keep out! Trespassers will be shot!" Sometimes we reject the very resources that God intended to bring healing and comfort to us. On some days *you* have to lower the drawbridge to let them in.

But suppose you're right: They *are* talking. Is that the end of the world? No! The absence of an old friend makes room for a new friend. Sometimes a forest must be thinned out to make room for the new trees.

Sometimes we must say goodbye to friends.

But don't be too hasty. Friendships stretch and strain, but most endure. You may be surprised. In this low time you'll find new proof of the strength of your friendships.

Give your friends time and space. Always leave the door slightly ajar. Remember, they may fear your rejection too. Share with them about your feelings, or else they will never know.

Give them some hints of how they might help you.

Be helpable!

The Sounds of Depression: "I Don't Care Anymore"

"O Lord, take away my life, for it is better for me to die than to live" (Jonah 4:3).

Jonah had crossed the threshold. Ironically, his words were not expressed in the belly of the whale but under a vine after he had preached in Nineveh, and after the people had actually repented. Jonah felt that God had disappointed him.

So we find him depressed and snarling at God's grace. Modern-day Jonahs can be found in every city and in every profession. Perhaps at the end of a particular day you have mumbled, "What's the use?" or "I don't care anymore!" But that statement implies that you once cared. What happened to change your mind?

Take Betty. Seven years of teaching in the inner city have exhausted her stockpile of resources. She suffers the "Sunday afternoon blues." Just knowing that she has to go to school the next day triggers her depression on Sundays. What happened to this dedicated teacher?

The realities of inner-city life have worn her down. Some of her colleagues gave up years ago. "Honey," one chides her, "they don't pay me enough money to take the worries home. When that 3:30 bell rings, I flip a little switch and that's it."

But Betty is designed to teach and to care. God designed all of us to work, to profit from our sweat and labor. Does Betty really "not care" anymore? Like many people, she spent much of her time trying to get situations and people and mates and children and institutions and bureaucracies to change.

Sometimes this means, "I want you to be *this* (or my) way." If they do not respond as we wish, we face a fork in the road or we throw in the towel.

The more we try, the more they resist. The more they resist, the more depressed we become.

The first time you said, "I don't care anymore," it may have surprised you. But the phrase becomes easier to say. In fact, it continues to get easier to say and to believe.

How many people have toiled in a shop or factory or office or classroom, bored and depressed, week after week, month after month?

- "I've put in too many years."
- "I've only got ten more years until I can retire."

Some are depressed for a gold watch and a savings bond. Jabez prayed, "Oh, that you would bless me and enlarge my territory! Let your hand be with me, and keep me from harm so that I will be free from pain" (1 Chronicles 4:10). Jabez prayed his prayer in a time of national crisis. And God "granted his request."

You *choose* to allow yourself to drift into apathy. You *choose* to mumble, "I don't care anymore!" You *choose* to remain at that point.

You've heard about the little boy who cried "Wolf! Wolf!" once too often. Maybe you've said, "I don't care anymore!" once too often. Now no one really believes you, and people are slow to respond to your pain and depression.

But your "I don't care" could stimulate another person's depression. Instead, perhaps God wants you to be the spark that ignites an "I *do* care" campaign.

Raj Choppra in *How to Make a Bad Situation Better* relates the story of his decision to accept a school superintendency that other men had turned down. He chose a school system in a city that had said, "We don't care." But those words were unacceptable to Choppra. He changed an entire school system by defusing the corporate depression and discouragement.

Choppra dared to believe that people who said "I don't care anymore" really *did* care or *could* care again. His "I do care" campaign brought new life to an ailing school system.[7] His principles will work in your life too.

Your last "I don't care" has possibly stimulated your current depression. I think you *do* care. Caring is one way to avoid depression. Next time you start to say, "I don't care..." don't finish the statement.

> **It isn't the load that weighs us down—but how we carry the load and how long.**

The Sounds of Depression: "You'd Cry Too"

Have you ever met one of those people who are tuned in to themselves? In the *me-first* age, they are everywhere. It doesn't matter what button or station selector you punch, you get the same. They proclaim, "*My* me is more important than *your* me!"

Me-firsters make good depressed people. If the world revolves around me, any turmoil must reverberate the earth as well. Other people have their own agendas and needs; most will reject your claims to preferred treatment.

Most me-firsters are good manipulators. After a couple of hints about their depression you're supposed to say—

- "Dear me!"
- "Oh my!"
- "How terrible!"

In some families it's high melodrama. Everyone knows their lines and their cues.

Helen is a typical me-firster. At one of my seminars she decided that I wasn't compassionate enough for widows. "I lost my husband," she began. "He was *brutally* murdered! And the men who killed him got off. Can you believe it?" The story went on and on, with every detail duly noted.

"I'm sorry," I replied.

"Is that *all?*" she demanded.

"Yes. How long ago did this happen?"

"Seven years ago. Can you believe it?"

"No, I can't. I can't believe that you would live 'on hold' for seven years."

"I loved my husband."

"Then let go."

I decided to push ahead. "Where is his underwear?"

"In the third drawer."

"And his suits?"

"In the closet."

"And his watch?"

"On the nightstand."

"I want you to get some of those black plastic bags and load up all his stuff. Put the bags on the back porch. Then call the Salvation Army to come and get them."

I expected her to be angry, but she listened in amazement.

"Do you think I should?" she finally asked.

"If you want to get over your depression, yes. Besides, I think you should live. *Let go!*"

In *My Utmost for His Highest,* Oswald Chambers reminds us that we cannot choose the site of our martyrdom. Nor can we choose the cause.

It's tempting to believe that my accident, my surgery, my rape, my divorce, my drug-abused child, my alcoholic husband, my (fill in the blank) _____ is the world's *greatest* tragedy. Such statements are subtle appeals to our ego. God wants *you* to be a survivor and a thriver—not just to survive the tragedy and its accompanying depression but to thrive after it.

"Oh," you scowl. "You'd cry too if it happened to you!"

That's true—I would probably cry. But we can learn to not allow the tragedy to imprison us in the dark pit of depression. We can *choose* to live.

We can survive anyone or anything we choose to survive. That's right—*we choose.* Good people, over the years, build such strong relationships as mates that some have moved God to second place. The mate has taken the place that God should occupy. Because we place such a premium on marriage today, we overlook the threat. Yet, John warned, "Dear

31

children, keep away *from anything* that might take God's place in your hearts'' (1 John 5:21 TLB).

Nothing other than God can be first in your life. Nothing.

Because of those acceptable "idols" we become depressed. Deep within ourselves we discover the inability of these cherished idols to meet our needs. One songwriter wrote, "Take the things that I hold dear . . ." Easy to sing, but hard to mean!

You can survive your loss. Eleanor Roosevelt may have been the nation's First Lady, but she wasn't FDR's. Yet after her husband's death she gave the rest of her life to the nation. The years *after* Franklin were years of great achievement for her.

How different from the widowhood of Mary Todd Lincoln (Mrs. Abraham Lincoln). She spent her last years on outrageous shopping sprees, battling Congress for bigger appropriations to liquidate her debts. Finally she was committed to the Cook County Lunatic Hospital.

What made the difference? Each was a widow of a much-beloved president, but *each made a choice.* Eleanor Roosevelt chose to survive and to thrive. Mary Todd Lincoln chose to whine.

It is appropriate to cry. But it is also appropriate to let go and live.

GOAL 2 ❖ RECOGNIZING YOUR DEPRESSION

The Value of Depression

Americans have worked hard to eliminate the word *suffering* from their vocabularies. Elizabeth Skoglund quipped, "We Americans with our fast answers, marathon therapy sessions, pills for every psychic twinge, and...facile spiritualizations of problems have developed a shallowness in our approach to pain and its resultant depression." She quoted one woman:

> For a person to assume that his life must consist of stepping from success to success is like a fool who stands next to a building site and shakes his head because he cannot understand why people dig deep down when they set out to build a cathedral. God builds a temple out of each man's soul, and in my case He is just starting out to excavate the foundations. It is my task to offer myself to His excavations.[8]

Because we stigmatize the depressed we have to ignore the value of the experience. For many people depression has been a path, somewhat unavoidable, to spiritual maturity and psychological growth. It is seldom a path willingly chosen. But this trail has led some to spiritual greatness.

- If depression depletes our arrogance—
- If depression reduces our pride—
- If depression brings us closer to those we love—
- If depression draws us closer to God—

then depression will have been valuable.

In the midst of any pain, God's embrace reminds us that we are His, and that *nothing* can separate us from His love.

As a child you may have cried out, "Mother, where are you?" Then you heard those comforting words, "I'm *right here.*"

Forsaken? No. Never! Jesus has promised, "Never will I leave you; never will I forsake you" (Hebrews 13:5). Rather, He is thinking about you—now—even in your depression. He never looks the other way.

The same psalmist who questioned God's love later wrote, "How precious it is, Lord, to realize that you are thinking of me *constantly!*" (Psalm 139:17 TLB).

"Depression may not be something any of us would seek, but it is an emotion that can be used rather than wasted."
—Elizabeth Skoglund

The Eleventh Commandment

Some Christians have very vocally composed an eleventh commandment: *Thou shalt not be depressed.* They reason that since depression has become such a big problem, it is time to get tough and lay down the law. A simple maxim or a bulletin insert won't do: "Give 'em a commandment."

Such Christians overlook the fact that some people are disposed to depression. For example, Christians who grew up in homes with depressed parents are more likely to be depressed. Some just happen to be good at covering up their depression. I overheard one conversation that went like this:

"Do you ever get depressed?"

"Who, me? I've got Jesus!" The tone of voice implied that if *you* really had Jesus too, you wouldn't or couldn't be depressed.

Some Christians have accepted the notion that Christians should never be depressed. We would have a better understanding of depression if we regularly visited those who attend our churches. After being in a home, we come to know that family better. Some of us do not get depressed because we do not visit the home of a single mother barely making ends meet. Some do not understand the angry depression of senior citizens trying to survive on Social Security and a pension.

It's easy to say, "Don't be depressed" when you're not on a limited or fixed income. When you're employed it's easy to say to unemployed or underemployed people, "Don't be depressed." When you have a good marriage, it's difficult to understand the depression of a person trapped in a poor marriage.

Some Christians believe that if they say "Don't be depressed"often enough or loudly enough, the depression will evaporate. Rather, the more we try to deny depression, the more devastating the experience.

Depression is a reality. Depression affects saints and sinners, Catholics and Protestants, those who raise their hands and those who keep their hands by their sides during worship, young and old, male and female.

Depression is a basic part of the human experience and is "no respecter of persons." Today, in an era when people crave simple answers to complex problems, Christians need to be more caring.

Christians *do* get depressed.

A Who's Who of
Depressed People

Depressed? Welcome to the fraternity. Depression is almost as old as mankind. Surely Adam and Eve were depressed that first night outside the Garden.

Are you aware that some of the most talented, creative, productive people in history have wrestled with depression?

- Vincent van Gogh: first great impressionistic painter.
- Peter Tchaikovsky: composed the classic Nutcracker Suite and other great Russian symphonies.
- Wolfgang Mozart: *the* musical genius of his day.
- Robert Schumann: great romantic composer.
- Ernest Hemingway: wrote *Old Man in the Sea* and other great novels.
- Fyodor Dostoyevski: author of *Brothers Karamazov* and the epic *Crime and Punishment*.
- Theodore Roosevelt: President of the United States.
- F. Scott Fitzgerald: American novelist.
- James Forrestal: first Secretary of Defense.
- Charles Spurgeon: great expository preacher.
- David Brainerd: first missionary to the American Indians.

One creative man, Robert Burton, authored *The Anatomy of Melancholy,* a classic in its day. As a refuge from his own depression Burton wrote about other people's depression.

Many great leaders, like Winston Churchill, learned to discipline their depression. He explained, ''I did my work,

I sat in the House of Commons, but black depression settled in on me."

If these great men, movers and shakers of their day, struggled with depression, why should you be exempt? The Scripture reminds us, "No temptation has seized you except what is common to man" (1 Corinthians 10:13).

Thanks to historians, we know something of the emotional pain felt by such superachievers. But remember that many of these came to their significant achievements only *after* or *through* their depression.

So, 200 years after his death, Mozart's music still brings delight to millions of listeners. Sometimes a depressed person simply has to get on with life's agenda.

A Who's Who of Depressed Saints

Paul, from a jail cell, gently pleaded, "Remember my chains." Paul's chains could have been an embarrassment. Rather, "because of my chains" Paul acknowledged that some people had become believers. By wearing the chains, Paul eliminated the stigma from subsequent generations of believers who would be imprisoned for their faith.

Hebrews 11 has been termed "the Who's Who of Faith." Through faith, these spiritual giants—

- conquered kingdoms.
- administered justice.
- gained what was promised.
- shut the mouths of lions.
- quenched the fury of the flames.
- escaped the edge of the sword.
- had their weakness turned into strength.

Reread that last phrase: *"had their weakness turned into strength."* Weakness among these spiritual giants?

These greats didn't have an easy life. They were jeered, flogged, chained, imprisoned, stoned, sawed in two, persecuted, and mistreated. In fact, "They wandered in deserts and mountains, and in caves and holes in the ground" (Hebrews 11:38). Are we to assume that they faced no psychological pain?

Jonah must have been depressed in the slimy darkness of the whale's belly.

Jeremiah must have been depressed in the muddy dampness of a cistern.

Joseph must have been depressed in the moldy prison cell.

Those who argue that "Christians don't get depressed!" have to ignore some strong biblical biographies. The writers of the Scriptures, under the direction of the Holy Spirit, spoke the truth, and we see a lot of blemishes in biblical heroes. We can conclude, if we uphold the inerrancy of Scripture, that the Holy Spirit wanted us to know the details of these men's struggles and failures as well as their achievements.

We can sense David's depression after the death of his handsome but rebellious son, Absalom. David covered his face and cried aloud, "O my son Absalom! My son, my son Absalom! If only I had died instead of you!" (2 Samuel 18:33). David's depression could not be contained in words. At times he didn't talk; he wept; he repeated himself; he ignored meals. But he *survived*.

If we listen closely we can sense Jesus' depression in His groan, "My God! My God! Why have *You* forsaken me?" I believe Jesus understands our depression because He Himself experienced depression. Therefore He sees no reason to be "ashamed to call us brothers." The author of Hebrews reminds us that Jesus was "made like his brothers in every way" (2:17) and is "touched by the feelings of our infirmities" (4:15 KJV).

For a long time I read that He is "touched . . . with our infirmities." But that's not what the passage says. "He is touched *with the feeling* of our infirmities." He is now our Advocate at the Father's right hand. He now says, "Yes, I remember."

Jesus came and lived among us so that He could understand us, so that He could remember our infirmities. He died as an adult in order to understand us.

Saints are not immune from depression. The words of the old gospel hymn underscore the point:

Some through the waters, some through the flood;
Some through the fire, but all through the blood;
Some through great sorrows, but God gives a song,
In the night season, and all the day long.[9]

The author deliberately placed "night season" first. In every believer's life there are night seasons. But those seasons can be turned into strength (Hebrews 11:34).

Walking Through
the Valley

Depression can be endured and survived. But the reality is clear: All of us must walk through the "valley of the shadow of death." We read Psalm 23 at funerals, but it has as much to do with depression as with death. "The shadow of death" is that mood that leads many people to moan, "I wish I were dead." There is a valley where there are shadows, and all of us have to journey through it.

Why do believers go through depression? Harold L. Bussell in *Unholy Devotion: Why Cults Lure Christians* cites four reasons. He says that evangelicals who try to deny their emotions end up as cult bait.[10]

First, we live in a world that has been devastated by the fall of man. Adam's sin has psychological results as well as genetic and spiritual ones. Some Christians are more prone to physiological diseases, some to psychological, a few to both.

Second, life is influenced by unseen spiritual forces. Satan may appeal to your mental arena rather than offer a sexual temptation. In any case, he will attempt to sabotage God's redemptive work in you. It's like a game show: Satan chooses the category in which he will tempt you.

Third, our actions have consequences. When you throw a rock into a pond, a ripple results. The bigger the rock, the bigger the ripple. Consequences, good and bad, result from our choices. Some of us have made choices which made us more temptable and thus more subject to depression.

For example, workaholics push their bodies beyond reasonable limits. Their choice to overwork sets up fatigue, which makes them vulnerable to depression.

Others may have made sexual choices. By saying yes to a level of sexual temptation, they underwrote the guilt that followed the behavior. Now they face depression because they said yes and fear that the next time they won't be able to say no. What if they should become pregnant or get venereal disease? Choices fuel depression.

Fourth, God allows difficulties to come into our lives—

- to test us.
- to challenge us.
- to strengthen us.
- to spark our growth.
- to cultivate our maturity.

The psalmist recognized this and wrote, "It was good for me to be afflicted so that I might learn your decrees" (Psalm 119:71). Often we learn the most from what we experience.

Jacob had to flee from his brother's anger because he had made a choice to deceive his father; now he had inherited the unpleasant consequences. On his journey to Uncle Laban, he paused. With a rock for a pillow, he drifted off to sleep. Some of us would have been too uptight to have slept. In fact, with Esau hot on our trail we would have tried to put as much distance between us as possible. But Jacob chose to rest.

A Texas ranger in the days of the Wild West became lost in a thicket of trees along a river bottom. Alarmed by the potential threat of Indians, he decided that prayer would help. But the ranger knew only one prayer: "Now I lay me down to sleep." He stopped. Sleep? That was the last thing he wanted to do in the presence of Indians.

Yet, since it was the only prayer he knew, he decided that a child's prayer would be better than no prayer. He slept safely. Later the ranger said that praying made him feel better "though that particular one didn't seem quite right at the moment.''[11] Sometimes our prayers don't seem right, but the Lord understands.

The experience for that ranger and for Jacob was the same: ''Surely the Lord is in this place, and I was not aware of it'' (Genesis 28:16).

In your depression, the Lord is present. You, like Jacob, are probably not aware of all the ways He has helped and guarded you. He has not and will not abandon you. Nor will He ever growl, ''Snap out of it!''

> **Trying to remove a symptom appears an easier route than focusing on the source of the symptoms.**
>
> **—John Drakeford**

Real Christians
Do Get Depressed

The early church was often buffeted by heresy—not always of the outrageous variety, either. Heresy is often accepted by many people because it contains an element of truth. Paul had Timothy stay in Ephesus to counteract certain men who taught false doctrines and devoted themselves to myths. Because of their influence, some had "wandered away...and turned to meaningless talk" (1 Timothy 1:6).

"Meaningless talk" is still with us—slogans, cliches, catchy phrases, half-truths. What could be more damaging to our spiritual well-being than the allegation "Real Christians don't get depressed"? It's like the slogan "Real men don't eat quiche." Says who? A lot of men eat quiche and a lot of Christians get depressed.

It's one thing when Satan accuses us, but how much more painful when a brother or sister accuses us! We can become so threatened by our humanity that we deny our depression.

Depression is feared by many Christians. Rather than "stalk their terror" they settle for simple solutions.

Don't let anyone "take away your faith." Christians *do* get depressed.

J. Edgar Hoover, as head of the FBI, did not have a good track record against the Mafia because he pretended there was no such thing. Christians have the option of pretending, but when that happens, the pain worsens and depression gets the upper hand.

Admit your depression. The God who knows your name already knows about your depression. Why not dare to believe that God will bring people and resources into your life to help you survive and thrive? He wants you, however, to be gentle with yourself.

Some people go around as "fire extinguishers" dousing other people's depression. But a *real* believer recognizes the pain of another Christian: "Carry each other's burdens, and in this way you will fulfill the law of Christ" (Galatians 6:2). Yes, your depression may inconvenience me or irritate me or perhaps frighten me, but I am your brother. I cannot ignore your need.

People will mouth platitudes, but the intensity with which they mumble does not guarantee accuracy.

Pretend is a game for children.

Real Christians *do* get depressed.

It's No Sin
To Be Depressed

Surely it has happened to you: Someone, perhaps a total stranger, has snapped at you, "It's a sin to be depressed!"

It was not so much the words as the tone of voice that hurt you. And you were probably more depressed after he or she left.

Well, depression *might* be a sin.

But *always* a sin? No.

If God had thought depression was a sin, He certainly would have said so. Christians must be cautious in speaking for God.

Satan, on the other hand, knows that overenthusiastic and overzealous believers get carried away. Satan delights in hearing our platitudes on depression. Why? Because they wound with an intensity that he could never muster.

John wondered, "How can we set our hearts at rest" in the midst of the accusations? How can we know the truth? He declared, "God is *greater* than our hearts, and he knows everything" (1 John 3:20).

Yes, God knows that some of His children are depressed. But because He knows, He understands.

"But why do people say such hurtful things to me?" Don Baker, a pastor who struggled with depression, explains, "It is impossible for those who have never been depressed to fully understand the deep, perplexing pain that depression causes."[12]

However, it might be a sin *to remain* depressed. God will bring resources (people, tracts, sermons, magazine articles, cassettes) to help us tolerate if not eliminate our depression.

Yet He will not force-feed us or threaten us. If we choose to remain depressed, He will not interfere.

David Brandt raises four areas in which a depressed person should ask questions.

- *Awareness*: "Am I depressed? To what degree? Why? Has this happened before?"
- *Motivation*: "What am I gaining by being depressed? Am I being excused from certain responsibilities?"
- *Decision*: "Am I going to continue to be depressed?"
- *Actions*: "What actions can *I* take to reduce or eliminate my depressions?"[13]

The debate on the sinfulness of depression will continue. Yet Baker reminds us "that countless Christians who know [that] their position in Christ is firm and who appreciate his gift of grace, through depression learn the sufficiency of His grace."[14]

The question is: *Are you willing to learn that sufficiency?*

It's no sin to be depressed, but it might be a sin to tell a depressed person, "It's a sin to be depressed!"

Archibald Hart explained the connection between sin and depression:

> Depression may be the consequence of sin, but the depression itself is not sin. If, for example, you have engaged in certain activities which are sinful, the depression that follows is a consequence of that sin. The activities are the sin and the depression that follows is a *symptom* of the sin and should be used to alert you to the fact that something is wrong.[15]

If you are depressed by all the imagined consequences of your sins, talk to the Lord about it. He is not a cruel God. He is the God who "does not treat us as our sins deserve." He is the God who looks into our depression. I think this is the beauty of Christ's dealing with Peter *after* the resurrection.

Peter must have remembered his denial of Jesus every time he saw a fire. But Jesus acted to diffuse that memory. When Peter had gone fishing, Jesus came to the shore and built a fire. Then He called to them.

After that moment, every time Peter remembered a fire, he remembered Jesus cooking fish and His words, ''Feed My lambs.''

If Jesus didn't treat Peter the way he deserved, He won't treat you the way you deserve (or think you deserve). It is Satan who cackles during your videotape replays and whispers, ''One of these days...''

Do yourself a favor: Memorize Psalm 103:10. You'll find it a great antidepressant!

Recognizing Your Type: Endogenous Depression

Endogenous depression is a biochemical disturbance in your hormones and brain chemicals. This depression comes from *within* rather than from external circumstances.

Three thousand years ago the psalmist said that we are "fearfully and wonderfully made." Scientists are daily proving the accuracy of that statement.

For example, significant breakthroughs have been made with substances called amino neurotransmitters or chemical messengers between brain cells.

Think of a bridge connecting two islands. Neurotransmitters create complex chemical interactions that control our behaviors, feelings, and thoughts. They do this by transferring nerve impulses from one brain cell to another.

Have you ever been frightened? Your heart beat rapidly and a substance called adrenaline was pumped through your bloodstream. In car accidents a 95-pound woman has been able to pick up one end of a car. Why? Because of the power of the adrenaline.

Similar chemicals are at work when you are depressed. Serotonin, for example, is linked to drowsiness. Some researchers think that high concentrations of serotonin in the brain account for the loss of energy and fatigue so common in depression.

Another substance related to depression is norepinephrine. If this substance is not being released into the central nervous system, a person is depressed. Through chemicals called tricyclics the brain is urged to manufacture and release more norepinephrine into the central nervous system.

Depression can be stabilized and reduced by drugs. Endogenous depression is one demonstration that depression cannot be automatically labeled sin. If you have a shortage of serotonin, you become depressed.

Stop and think: Are you personally responsible for your serotonin level? Is there *anything* you can do about the present level in your body? Hardly.

Simply because we are fearfully and wonderfully made, we are subject to depression created by chemical imbalances. But why would a loving God make us vulnerable to depression based on chemical imbalances?

Well, if we had "joy-joy-joy" all the time, why would we need God? God permits us to experience depression for a good reason.

> Depression is like pain. While pain is inconvenient, it is a warning signal, essential for our survival. We wouldn't ask, "Why does God allow me to experience pain?" If I felt no pain, I'd be killed the first day I walked out my front door.

> God has also created me with the ability to experience depression so that I can have an important warning system to tell me when things are wrong. But He doesn't allow me to be depressed as a form of punishment.[16]

If Christians were immune from depression, a lot of folks would want to be Christians just for the fringe benefits.

It's true that the Bible says, "His yoke is easy and His burden is light." But depression is a reality: God permits depression. He also gives wisdom to researchers to develop drugs to help manage those biochemical imbalances. He gives doctors the wisdom to prescribe those "helpers."

In time there will be more breakthroughs. But if you need chemical help with depression, by all means get it! And thank God for His provision for you.

Recognizing Your Type:
Reactive Depression

Loss begins early in life, when we misplace or lose a favorite possession or toy. On special occasions my family used to go to the Blue Boar Cafeteria. I liked the place because they gave balloons to children.

But I have not forgotten the first balloon I lost. I was playing in the backyard when the balloon slipped through my fingers. I watched in horror as it lifted into the bright afternoon sky. I screamed and I pleaded, but the balloon continued being a balloon.

Worse, no one gave me his balloon to replace mine. "It's gone!" my brother concluded. How's that for sympathy?

We have to learn to lose things, persons, or objects that are valuable to us. Loss creates reactive depression. The greater the attachment to a person or object, the deeper the loss and depression.

However, by adulthood, lost balloons seem minor complaints. Yet the process is the same: We stand by helpless to recover the object or person.

So our task is to come to terms with the loss. Often we have the capacity to replace an object. Suppose you have an auto accident and "total" your car. In a few days you will probably have replaced it through insurance. Although you will miss the old car (especially if it was paid off!), you will adjust.

However, some things have such meaning to us that we cannot replace them. Suppose you break a china cup and saucer that had belonged to your great-grandmother. That could easily cause depression because it is not replaceable.

Then we mourn; the low mood hangs in there. But slowly, through a process called erasure, the memory fades and loses its capacity to provoke pain and depression over this particular loss.

But some people can't get over their loss easily or, in some cases, at all. A lifelong grief triggers a long-term depression.

David and his men had suffered severe loss. Their town, Ziklag, had been sacked and burned. Their wives and children had been taken captive. Listen to their depression:

> David and his men wept aloud *until they had no strength left* to weep. . . . David was greatly distressed because the men were talking of stoning him; each one was bitter in spirit because of his [missing] sons and daughters (1 Samuel 30:4,6).

David not only wept for his two wives, Ahinoam and Abigail. He also wept for an "abstract" loss—his position and status with his men: They were talking of stoning him. What an abrupt change! In the previous chapter David had received glowing compliments. Achish had said, "You have been as pleasing in my eyes as an angel of God" (2 Samuel 29:9).

No wonder David was depressed! He had hit "the big dip." David turned to the Lord "and found strength in the Lord his God" (30:6). So must you in your loss, whatever the scale.

Archibald Hart identified four categories of loss.[17]

Real or *concrete*. Losses of tangible objects, such as things we can handle or see:
- We drop and break our camera.
- We have an automobile accident.

Either may be replaced, at a price.

Abstract. Intangible losses, which are just as real:
- We lose an election or ballgame.
- We lose a friendship over a misunderstanding.
- Our favorite restaurant closes.

Hart explains, "Such things don't really exist 'out there' but achieve reality only in ourselves." For example, that favorite restaurant is a scene of so many good memories. You choose to go there when you want to celebrate a special occasion or need a lift. Now where will you go? In time another restaurant may take it's place, but for now it is a painful loss.

Imagined. Losses created by our imaginations:
- We *think* a friend has snubbed us.
- We *think* a colleague is avoiding us.
- We *think* people are talking about us.

One question will dissolve depression based on imagined losses: *"Have these things actually happened?"* For example, I was excited about signing a book contract with a certain publisher. On the day I was to be notified, the editor didn't call. So I called. His secretary reported, "Something's come up. He'll get back to you." Two weeks passed. My imagination created all sorts of "logical" but negative explanations, the worst one being that he didn't want my book (which means the publisher didn't want me). Then my mind filled in all sorts of rejections. Bang! Instant depression.

A month later I discovered that the "something's come up" was the death of the editor's mother. The editor was away for two weeks, and when he returned there were certain priorities that *had* to be dealt with—the current production schedule, for example.

The fact that I was not his top priority did not reflect on me or my writing. But I *imagined* that it did.

Finally, there are

Threatened losses. Potential real or abstract losses which have not and may not happen:[18]
- The man waiting for test results to come back.
- The woman who waited two weeks and hasn't heard from the job interview.

It may not happen, but then it *may* happen.

Of the four, Hart believes that threatened losses are the toughest because of the element of reality in the threat. "You can't avoid the depression completely because there is the possibility of a real loss. On the other hand, you can't accept your loss, complete your grieving and resolve the depression, because the loss hasn't actually happened." So you are in limbo.

Why should this be a problem for Christians?

- We live in a society that doesn't communicate clearly.
- We play a lot of games with each other.
- We send hidden messages.
- We don't send or receive clear messages.
- We avoid telling each other the truth.

So, in trying to make sense of the puzzle, we sometimes put the wrong pieces together.

Reactive loss, particularly to tangible objects, is a special problem in a consumer-oriented, materialistic society. No Amish farmer, for example, ever gets depressed because his car won't start. Why not? Because the Amish do not own cars.

But if his prize horse should become lame, that would depress him immensely.

Those who base their worth on the loot and trinkets they have accumulated are predisposed to reactive loss and consequent depression. If you've got it, you can lose it—or someone could steal it.

Reactive depressions are responses to day-to-day problems.

Recognizing Your Type: Neurotic Depression

Some people cannot deal with the pressures of daily life, so they become hermits. They reject the slightest intrusion or inconvenience. Hart defines neurotic depression as "lifestyle responses to the stresses and anxieties of life which have built up over a long period of time."[19] These are not temporary bouts or episodes of depression.

Psychologists diagnose this as *dysthymic disorder*. It involves moodiness or loss of interest/pleasure in all, or almost all, usual activities and pastimes.

The depression persists. However, the depression may be broken by periods of normal mood lasting a few days to a few weeks, but no more than a few months at a time.

The person experiences at least three of the following:

- Insomnia.
- Lower energy level or chronic tiredness.
- Feeling inadequate, loss of self-esteem, or self-depreciation.
- Decreased effectiveness or productivity at school, work, or home.
- Decreased attention, concentration, or ability to think clearly.
- Social withdrawal.
- Irritability or excessive anger.
- Inability to respond with apparent pleasure to praise or rewards.
- Less active or talkative than usual, feeling slowed down or restless.

- Fearfulness or crying.
- Recurrent thoughts of death or suicide.[20]

How many did you check? Regardless of the number checked, a neurotic depressed person remains in touch with reality.

What makes a person neurotic? Coleman says that the individual reacts to a distressing situation—

- with more than the usual amount of sadness

or

- fails to return to normal after a reasonable length of time.

Most people suffering from neurotic depression can identify what caused or triggered their depression. But they cannot always explain their *overreaction* to it.

However, three other factors may influence this individual: Low stress tolerance, rigid conscience development, and proneness to guilt feelings.

> Typically, the stress situation seems to center around an individual's Achilles' heel—that is, some stress situation that reactivates earlier conflict or trauma. For example, the death of one's husband may reactivate insecuritites and conflicts associated with the death of one's father years before.[21]

So the patient may feel anxious about more losses. "Who's next?" asks Betty after the death of father, husband, and a brother. Furthermore, these episodes may be triggered by the anniversary of a loved one's death.

In other cases, the depression results from anger or hostility. Betty, for example, had strong feelings toward her father. But as a Christian, she thought she had to repress them rather than admit them. However, by repressing the attitudes, she struggled with intense dreams and depression.

Then her father died. Now Betty deals with her grief and guilt. "What if people knew how you really felt about your father?'' her self-talk asks. This is also common for widows from bad marriages. They have the insurance money and social acceptance (as compared to that of a divorcee), but they have depression.

This kind of depression can be habit-forming. The neurotically depressed use their symptoms to force support and sympathy from others. Psalm 107 offers some fascinating insights into this pattern.

Verses 4-9 mention those persons ''who wandered in desert wastelands...hungry and thirsty,'' their lives ebbing away. When ''they cried out to the Lord,'' He delivered them from their distress.

However, the tenth verse identifies a rebellious people—individuals who had rejected the Word of God. They sat ''in darkness and deepest gloom, prisoners suffering in iron chains.'' Well, you may not be in iron chains, but you are suffering. Hope is from the same source. When they cried out to the Lord in their trouble, He saved them. God ''brought them out of darkness and the deepest gloom and broke away their chains'' (107:14).

If God can ''break down gates of bronze and cut through bars of iron,'' He can slice through the fog of your depression and set you free—*if* you want to be freed.

Is it time for you to let go of that loss which triggers your depression, to let go of that which chains you to the past?

Is it time to abandon your chains and your ashes for the dream that God has monogrammed for you?

Recognizing Your Type: Spiritual Depression

Depression has a lot of sources. As early as the fourth century B.C., physicians such as Hippocrates speculated on the sources of melancholia. Plutarch offered one explanation. The depressed man—

> looks on himself as a man whom the gods hate and pursue with their anger. . . . He has gone some way other than which the Divine Being. . .approves of. The festivals in honor of the gods give no pleasure to him but fill him rather with fear or fright.[22]

This book focuses primarily on *spiritual* depression rather than clinical. Such factors as superspirituality, sin, success, stress, self-centeredness, should-ness, and sensitivity will be examined. Christians can succumb to spiritual depression because of the gap between what they wish they were (or someone has told them they *ought* to be) and what they know they are.

Three elements encourage depression among Christians. First is the creation of a cadre of celebrity Christians.

You see this personality in brief settings—concerts, lectures, worship services—and you *assume* that what you see is typical of all their lives, 24 hours a day. You say, "If only I could be like _____." But you can't. Why? God doesn't create "juniors." There was no—

- Abraham, Jr.
- Isaac, Jr.
- Joseph, Jr.
- Paul, Jr.

Each person is called to be a unique gift of God.

Often the painful discovery that we can't be like a celebrity leads to depression. Maybe there is some gift of the Spirit that I need to receive...maybe that would make the difference. Maybe if I tried harder...

The more intense our desire to be like the celebrity, the deeper our depression. However, when God leads us to give up our desire through the nudging of the Holy Spirit, we then sense a glimpse of what He dreams for us. As long as we compare our imperfection with their alleged perfection, we will be depressed.

The emergence of religious television has been a tool to win many people to God's kingdom. But it has also been a producer of celebrity-consciousness. And celebrities, Christian or secular, become idols. We must admit—

> that we are the ones who want to believe that there is someone out there who is perfect. There seems to be an unquenchable longing to hope with all our hearts that someone is able to live this Christian life the way it is supposed to be lived. We can't live that way, but surely Chuck Swindoll or Amy Grant or Joni can. Please, God, tell us it's true.[23]

As long as we cling to celebrities (and express outrage if they tumble off the pedestal), it's hard to trust Jesus, who tells us that we are loved and forgiven, who promises us that someday we will be part of a new kingdom where failure and depression are no longer present.

Second, spiritual depression is encourged by our lack of knowledge of God's Word. "Thy Word have I hid in my heart," said the psalmist, "that I might not sin against God." When one is biblically illiterate, it's easy to be "blown about by every wind of doctrine." No wonder some Christians are always into the latest "teaching," even if it is heresy!

God's Word—not a celebrity of a book—confirms your uniqueness. Listen to these two spectacular promises:

"For I know the plans I have for you," declares the Lord,

"plans to prosper you and not to harm you, plans to give you hope and a future" (Jeremiah 29:11).

Fear not, for I have redeemed you; I have called you by name; you are mine (Isaiah 43:2).

There are no asterisks with either verse which say, *"Except for the depressed."*

The psalmist said, "May the words of my mouth [my self-talk] and the meditation of my heart be pleasing in your sight, O Lord, my Rock and my Redeemer" (Psalm 19:14). Can depression and accusing self-talk or secret-talk be pleasing to God? Can psychological pain, brought on by our choices, please Him?

There are times when God seems hidden. The psalmist groaned, "How long, O Lord? Will you forget me forever? How long will you hide your face from me? How long must I wrestle with my thoughts and every day have sorrow in my heart?" (Psalm 13:1,2).

Have you ever prayed such a prayer? I cannot tell you when your depression will end. But God is there, and He cares for you.

He may not come through in the manner you expect, nor will He always come through on your time schedule. Elijah, a great servant of God, survived—

a great and powerful wind which tore the mountains apart and shattered the rocks,
But the Lord was not in the wind.
Elijah survived an earthquake,
But the Lord was not in the earthquake.
Elijah survived a fire,
But the Lord was not in the fire.

But after the wind, the earthquake, and the fire came a gentle whisper (1 Kings 19:11,12). That was God. No wonder we are reminded to be still and know that He is God!

Recognizing Your Type: Learned Depression

One of the most quoted proverbs is, "Train up a child in the way he should go, and when he is old, he will not depart from it" (Proverbs 22:6 KJV). I doubt that one could be a parent and not have that Proverb well-memorized.

Psychologists are helping us gain new insights into the minds of children and the value of childhood. Jerome Kagan contends that we are like—

> a traveler whose knapsack is slowly filled with doubts, dogma, and desires during the first dozen years. Each traveler spends the adult years trying to empty the heavy load in the knapsack until he or she can confront the opportunities that are present each day.... Most adults carry their collection of uncertainties, prejudices and frustrated wishes into middle and old age trying to prove what must remain uncertain while raging wildly at ghosts.[24]

Generally the root of most adult depression traces back to childhood. Like exposure to certain diseases, it takes time to incubate. Then suddenly you've got the disease. But why do some people struggle with depression while their brothers and sisters, reared in the same home, escape? Simply, some people are more resistant than others.

"Honor your father and mother" to some people means, "Don't say anything bad about your parents, *ever*." If necessary, deny the truth. A lot of "Christian" homes are not good homes. A lot of Christian marriages are negative and sow seeds of pain into the linings of the next generation.

While psychoanalysis is on the wane, some people are fixated with their pasts. They have spent thousands of dollars and hours evaluating their childhoods. Every memory must take its turn under the microscope. They indict parents for sins of commission and omission. They explain their adult behavior as a consequence of some parental failure in childhood.

Look at the following inventory of family "heirlooms" that are passed along. Families appreciate such things as china, silver, watches, clocks, and quilts that have been in the family for years. But families also pass along emotional heirlooms.[25]

	ATTITUDE	STATE OF MIND
Belligerence	Chip on the shoulder.	Ready to fight or argue.
Excessive moodiness	Feeling down in the dumps.	Feeling that little is worthwhile.
Exaggerated worry	"What am I gonna do?"	Problems all the time.
Suspiciousness & mistrust	"Everyone's out to get me."	The world is full of dishonest people.
Selfishness & greed	"What's in it for me?"	A tendency to let others do it.
Helplessness & dependency	"But what can I do?"	Paralysis.
Poor emotional control		Exaggerated emotional outbursts.
Hypochondria	"I'm too sick."	Nursing minor ailments & experiencing imaginary symptoms.

How many of these are in your emotional repertoire?

By the time we become adults we've learned certain lines. As a result of practice it's hard to abandon some of these when our backs are to the wall. One researcher said that most adult emotional tension is a response to "earlier experiences which distorted normal emotional responses, and set us up with inappropriate and ineffective ways of dealing with life situations." So when we're weak, we choose from our arsenal.

Four factors promote learned depression.[26]

1. *A long and wearing siege of trouble, sickness, tragedy, and/or hard luck.* These condition people to be on constant alert and always trigger-happy. They expect woe so that woe can't sneak up on them.

2. *A constant air of doom and gloom in the home.* If a child grows up in a climate hearing about woe, fretting and complaining about the unfairness of it all, he may conclude that the world is like his home. He will be uncomfortable with happiness. He will expect trouble even if it has to be created.

3. *Neglect or rejection in childhood.* A child who is ignored or mistreated sometimes concludes that such treatment is deserved. He doubts his own positive virtues. In time, the self-depreciating child becomes the depressed adult who expects to be hurt and rejected. The child doubts his ability to make any relationship work. Why risk a relationship? They *might* reject me. Don't expect too much; that way you won't be disappointed.

4. *Constant scolding and criticism.* This endows the child with an overactive sense of guilt. He feels he's "no good" or "worthless" or "bad." He can't meet his parents' expectations: "Why can't you behave?" He doesn't know. The child may set up his own test to prove his parents wrong. But if he should fail, he becomes convinced: His parents were right all along.

In one family you have the passive child who adjusts and "goes with the flow." His brothers or sisters may be reactive and fight the system. They shrug off criticism. Some children are more psychologically or spiritually fragile and are more vulnerable to psychological stress. Others reject stress like water off a duck's back.

Most children have strong cravings for affection and acceptance that pushes them to desperate means in adult relationships.

Children closely observe parental relationships. They sense when one mate uses depression to manipulate the other mate. Eventually the child tries depression on for size. Thus depression is passed from one generation to the next.

As a believer you must remember that depression is a family affair. Myra Weissman of Yale says that if one of your parents was depressed, your chances for depression are two to three times greater than that of a child from a nondepressed-parent home.[27] If *both* parents were depressed, your odds are four to six times as great.

Depression can be learned and mimicked. But if it's learned, it can also be unlearned and abandoned. No one is chained to the past. *You can choose to be unchained from the past!*

GOAL 3 ❖ UNDERSTANDING YOUR DEPRESSION

Sources of Depression: Society

Depression is definitely influenced by society's pressures—

- to *be* something.
- to *do* something.
- to *own* something.
- to *achieve* something.
- to *prove* something.

If you fail in any of these standards, you naturally become depressed. The bigger the goal, the deeper the depression. "You're supposed to be successful."

It began when our forefathers walked down the gangplank. A significant number of them were not bluebloods but indentured servants who had agreed to work for seven years in exchange for their passage. Most left everything behind in the Old Country.

There was a lot of land in the colonies. The more land you owned, the colonists reasoned, the more "blessed" you were. They became locked in proving that they had been predestined by God.

Obviously there were some losers—people who struggled and existed, but that's about all. But then they couldn't complain, because it was God's will at work.

As evangelicals have become more affluent and as the affluent have been drawn into the born-again movement, our difficulties have increased. What's it like to park in your church's parking lot? "Ah, I see the Thompsons have a new car." Do you break into the doxology? Do you wonder, "Why didn't God bless us?"

The "prosperity gospel" has spurred the problem: "Name it and claim it." If you don't have the loot, it's because you don't have insights into the kingdom. So until you do, you're depressed because you have no prosperity to show.

If you buy into the shallow philosophies of this world, you get the consequences. Only a rat wins the rat race! One major by-product is reactive depression, triggered by a significant loss: death of a mate, divorce, or a major financial reverse.

Some people are depressed by the loss of their longings, fantasies, or wishes. When I worked at Sears in the catalog department, our Christmas catalog was commonly called "the Wish Book." Many adults and children marked pages and circled order numbers indicating that *this* is what I want Santa to bring me.

During the Christmas rush we sold out of some of the items, and we offered substitutes. Most were accepted; some were rejected. "But she has her heart set on it!" a mother would plead. "She'll be so disappointed! Can't you do something?"

Adults have their wish books too. We can almost savor how we'll feel when we have "it"—whatever it is.

Ironically, some things—essential to us, luxuries to most of the world—fuel our depression. More leads to more; attainment stimulates the desire for bigger or better. The battle lines for personal conflict are drawn between husband and wife, child and parent, friends and neighbors.

But I've come to a startling conclusion:

- I don't have to *do* anything!
- I don't have to *prove* anything!
- I don't have to *own* anything!
- I don't have to *achieve* anything!

Christ has done it all for me. He has freed me from the

wants and the *shoulds*. He has freed me from depression based on material trinkets. But if I accept the standards of this world, there will always be someone with—

- bigger or better.
- newer or improved.

Even if I get ahead, I am behind. If I realize I have more than most people in the world, I feel more ashamed about complaining because I don't have as much as I want or crave.

If I am going to avoid depression, I must choose to reject the materialistic standards of this world. I must reject the captivity—even couched in evangelistic jargon—of a society too enthused with materialism. I have to reject the secular philosophy embraced by many Christians:

- *Take* more.
- *Make* more.
- *Spend* more.
- *Get* more.

Otherwise I'll be on an economic treadmill that leads to depression. True, society has ways of recognizing its "Who's Who" winners. But so does God. Those who are kingdom-seekers rather than trinket-collectors will have their reward—in His time and on His scale.

> **Our society has a clever way of breeding depression but condemning those who succumb.**

Sources of Depression: Superspirituality

What is it about athletic competition that tempts us to abandon the really important things in life to stare in wonderment at these athletes? "How do they do it?" we wonder.

Some commentators only contribute to the problem. Television sportscasters think they must comment on every dive, every play, every routine. Worse, there seems to be a *but* or *however* or *if only* in their voice. *If only* the diver had done some minute gesture, *then* the dive would have been better. I'd like to see the sportscasters take off their blazers and try!

Now the athletes themselves are complaining about too many "perfect" scores. So the standards for the next Olympics or international competition will have to be tightened.

Some Christians want higher *spiritual* scores—in other words, perfection. The quest for spiritual perfection is a treadmill that saps our strength. Don Baker reminds us, "There are only three persons in the Godhead—and you are not one of them."[28] Yet we strive and struggle to meet the standards we have designed or that someone has imposed on us. This world wants perfection. We are humiliated by a boss or parent or mate or teacher, pushed out of the way with a "Here, I'd rather do it myself!" or an "Anyone could do better than you!"

Such scolding words are depression seeds planted in the soil of our lives, often at a point when we are helpless as well as embarrassed. Such seeds grow inside our spirits long after an apology. Some people struggle with intense feelings of inferiority, guilt, and worthlessness—emotions that fuel their depression.

The more you try to reach the standard, the more it eludes you. "Your brother made all A's. Why can't you do as well?" So you tried—hard. You could hardly wait to show your parents your report card. Then your dad scoffed, "They must have lowered the standards if *you* got all A's!"

Some people not only have high expectations, but they think they have to achieve them in "Lone Ranger" style. They avoid individuals who might help them attain or reassess the standard. Too often our achievement goals are exaggerated and therefore impossible to attain.

Motivational speakers suggest, "You can achieve anything your mind can conceive!" Then they parade a few super-achievers as examples. We strain to catch every word of their "This is how I made it big!" speech. But we ignore the real question: *Is the goal worthy of my investment?* At what price will I achieve the goal?

Bill was one such superachiever. He tried harder. He put in the hours. He made the goals. But he lost his family in the process. He had reminded himself all along that he was doing it "for the family." But his family couldn't wait for Bill; they needed a husband and father in the meantime.

I could head for the swimming pool every day. I could dive until my bloodstream is chlorinated, but I will *never* qualify for the Olympic team. That is not a negative thought. That, my friend, is reality!

But it is possible for someone to manipulate me into accepting his goal for me and thereby sentence me to bouts of depression because I cannot reach that goal. Every time I try to dive, a minefield of depression will explode.

I grieved with some of our Olympic athletes who lost despite the sacrifices and the rigorous training.

Taking it one step further, you may be depressed because by striving for perfection, unrealistic goals dominate your thinking. Are the psychological bruises and wounds you have accumulated worth it?

God has accepted you as you are. Relax—He even likes you! There is nothing you can do to get Him to like you more than He already does. You have been made worthy through Jesus Christ. Jesus said, "You did not choose me, but I chose you" (John 15:16). Those words free us from the chafing yoke of perfectionism.

But I weep for the depressed and bruised who keep trying and failing, and who bitterly denounce themselves for each failure. I weep for those who have abandoned their faith and their dreams because they cannot "measure up," who are one ounce more human than angelic.

Depression is the immediate by-product of perfectionistic strivings. Too many people have gotten locked into the cycle of defeated living by trying to reach unrealistic goals. How quickly they convene the grand jury to indict themselves!

God, through His Son, made a commitment to us "while we were still sinners" (Romans 5:8). He is the patient God who is still God in the midst of our messes. When we fail to catch the pass, He is the God who throws to us again. But He is also the God who grins when we catch the pass.

Sources of Depression: Sin

It's about 50-50, I suppose. There are those who would say, "Counseling is the answer to depression." An equally vocal group would argue, "Counseling? You don't need counseling! Confess it, brother. Confess the sin of depression!"

I've said it before, but it bears repeating: Depression may not be a sin in itself, but it may be a sin to *remain* depressed.

Well-meaning but misguided "pop theologians" or "amateur psychologists" have taken a smattering of psychological jargon and cliches and have created even more depression. Perhaps you are one of their victims.

Let's be honest: Sin does lead to depression. Depression can lead to sin. What about the promiscuous woman torn by her guilt? She continues to choose actions that only stimulate and expand her depression. She's like the man, alarmed at the size of his Visa bill, who keeps on charging anyway.

But the same woman, if she has overfocused on her loneliness, may be quicker to say yes to fornication. It's the cycle of unvictorious living, and its most immediate by-products are guilt and depression.

There are detectives in the body of believers—amateur private eyes who take their assignments seriously. "Unconfessed sin!" they conclude. "There's *got* to be unconfessed sin! We've got to root it out! Out come the magnifying glasses. No clue is too small or insignificant. Where will the trail end? With more depression.

Many Christians are depressed because they have magnified their sins, or else they keep tripping up on some besetting sin. This can lead to spiritual pride: "See how sensitive I am!" Yet the Word is clear: "If [or *when*] we confess our sins, he is faithful and just and will forgive us" (1 John 1:9).

If I am depressed because I keep repeating the same sin, won't God get weary of me? No!

Confession is good for the soul, according to popular thought. Confession frees us from the weight of our depression. God seeks an honest relationship with all His children. What violates that?

Past sin. By replaying old videotapes of our sins, failures, and mistakes, we create depression. Some videotapes always seem to be "cued-up" for immediate airing. Yet the Word is clear: "There is *now no condemnation*" from God's point of view. Can God lie? If He said *no condemnation*, that means not even a trace.

If God forgives me, I must forgive myself as well. This is not being self-indulgent; it's accepting the gift of God in my life.

"But what about the consequences?" Yes, there may be unpleasant consequences to our choices. However, there may not be, or at least not the consequences that we expect or fear.

Present sin. Some people are depressed because they choose to sin; they choose actions which are not pleasing to God, actions that grieve the Holy Spirit. Paul asked, "Shall we go on sinning so that grace may increase?" (Romans 6:1). But try this paraphrase: "Shall we go on sinning so that *depression* may increase?"

Hear Paul's answer to the first: "By no means! We died to sin; how can we live in it any longer?" (6:2). "Therefore do not let sin reign in your mortal body so that you obey its evil desires" (6:12).

Future sin. "But what if I repeat the same sin?" Pro football players are paid big money to catch passes. The more intense the game, the higher the expectation of the owners and the fans. But sometimes they miss as many as they catch. Do they turn in their uniforms? No. They go back to the huddle and run another play.

We must be alert to those tendencies which lead to certain sins. This means being alert to whatever would tempt us, rob us of our victory, and increase our depression.

But we can never anticipate tomorrow. Jesus said, "Do not worry about tomorrow, for tomorrow will worry about itself" (Matthew 6:34). David Augsburger said in *Caring Enough to Forgive—Caring Enough Not to Forgive—*

- Let what was... be gone!
- Let what will be... come!
- Let what is now... be!

Sin, whether past, present, or future, has a remedy: Confession. Once we have confessed, we must rely on the words of the One who said, "I do not condemn you." So then why condemn yourself? That only leads to depression.

Do yourself a big favor—trust Jesus.

Our sins are seldom as objectionable as the methods we think up to hide them!

Sources of Depression:
Stress

You think you're depressed. How would you like to have had Ezra's responsibility? He was chosen to take exiles to Jerusalem, plus 25 tons of silver and almost four tons of gold. Just putting up with the finicky children of Israel would be stressful. But what about the enemies and bandits along the way?

Stress is a by-product of a success/achievement-oriented society. Harry Truman used to say, "If you can't stand the heat, get out of the kitchen!" Stress creates depression. The fantasies, the dreams, the expectations, or the "what ought to be's" when compared to what we are leaves a gap that has to be spanned. Depression becomes the bridge.

As a college admissions officer, I talked to thousands of students who wanted to be doctors. I cautioned the students that premed was a stress-oriented major. The competition was extremely tight for med school. *Every* test became important; every less-than-the-best sparked depression. Some students made it, but others changed eventually to science education and slowly let the air out of their dreams.

The University of Louisville Medical School has a unique program to reduce the stress and depression of first-year med students and their families. The program started in 1981 when a depressed med student remarked to a lab partner that he had a pistol in his safety deposit box and was considering killing himself.

That fellow student "tattled" to Dr. Leah Dickstein,

a psychiatrist who counsels medical students. After treatment and counseling, the depressed student left the med school and has found success in another profession.

Several years ago a similar thing happened at a Southern university. However, the student's roommates chose silence, fearing the student might be expelled. Then the student leaped out a twelfth-story window and ended his brilliant future.

Stress kills—but before it kills it mangles. How many times have you asked, "Is it *really* worth it?" The depression is because of the "gap." Rather than face the problem, we mutter, "Maybe if I try a little harder..."

It isn't the load that weighs us down—it's how long we carry the load and how we carry that load.[29]

Some of us never get the bag unloaded, and we swat at the ghosts who whisper, "You'll never amount to anything." We endure the job a little longer, trying to "prove something to someone." Slowly the stress or depression gains on us.

How many businessmen have lain in motel rooms, depressed because they missed their daughter's piano recital or son's ballgame? How many have hated themselves for saying, "Sorry, the company comes first"?

David, a salesman, realizes that if he is to make "the good times roll" for his wife and children, he has to make *this* sale, *this* goal. But sometimes David misses a sure sale, and depression tracks him to a lonely motel room. Then there's always the lounge for a few drinks.

Murray has put in 15 years with a company and has worked hard to be the director of sales. Slowly he has discovered that he can't make things happen anymore. The boss isn't going to change, and now everything is covered with the residue of depression.

Depression can be a good gift. Depression can be a God-given time-out from the pressure and from the nagging question, "Is it really worth it?"

Ezra became a great leader because he recognized God

in the dark times of exile. He said, "Our God gives light to our eyes and a little relief in our bondage." In words that his depressed listeners could understand, Ezra said, "Though we are slaves, our God has not deserted us in our bondage" (Ezra 9:8,9).

Sources of Depression:
The Shoulds

Urban T. Holmes insisted that each individual must confront three questions:

- What should I *do*?
- What should I *not* do?
- What should I do *first*?[30]

There aren't enough resources to meet all the requests that you face. This is one reason why women are becoming more susceptible to depression. Women who work are supposed to be able to "get it all done" and still be "supermoms." In the twentieth century, the unpardonable sin is to fail to gratify your child's needs. Every parent wants to be a good parent.

Many Christians read the latest evangelical-celebrity bestseller describing that individual's climb to sainthood. A few hint, "This is what you *should* do if you want to be like me."

Lillian Thrasher struggled with what she *should* do. Ten days before her wedding she realized that God wanted her to break the engagement. God wanted her instead to go to Africa as a missionary. Ten days before she was to marry a fine minister she loved? Should she obey? For Lillian, there was no question.

After her arrival in Egypt, a dying woman gave Lillian her baby. "Take care of her." Lillian took the baby back to the missionary compound, where the baby cried frantically and persistently for ten days, enormously disturbing the other missionaries. "Take it back," the senior missionary ordered.

Lillian looked at the tiny, malnourished girl and pondered her decision. Then she disobeyed.

Out of that courageous act of obedience to God and disobedience to man came the Assiout Orphanage. In a day without financial support, an unmarried American woman survived and operated a faith orphanage. She rode her donkey from village to village, begging for food for the children. Sometimes the temperatures reached 125 degrees, but still she traveled. Often the only safe place to spend the night was a jail cell.

On many occasions there was no food for the next meal. What should she do? She always prayed and believed and waited.

When more and more orphans appeared on her doorstep, she pondered, "Which ones do I turn away?" Yet she continued to make room for each new arrival, first in her compound and then in her heart. Even when friends emphatically urged her not to take in any more children, Lillian retorted, "Will Jesus stop supplying our needs because I take in a new baby who has just lost its mother?"

In 1961 the criticism intensified and no doubt led to temporary depression for Lillian. American supporters wanted her to turn these Moslem orphans into Christians. Lillian wrote:

> I have been told that I have not raised enough preachers and that I have too many children. Who knows what God feels about this?
>
> I wish I were able to give you some wonderful reports to encourage you, but our work is so different from most works. It takes a lifetime for one of my babies to grow up and become important, if ever. . . . Books may be destroyed, papers may be burned or lost. The seeds planted in the heart of a child may lie dormant for years and then suddenly spring into life.
>
> Sometimes I get my eyes on results, especially when I read of all those wonderful meetings where thousands are saved

and brought to God. Then I begin to wonder if all the "glory" belongs to the preacher . . . . Anyway, our job is planting, and it is God who will give the increase.[31]

Many missionaries would have abandoned Assiout, but not Lillian Thrasher. She waited 17 years for the spiritual breakthrough. Then she exuberantly wrote:

Can you imagine my joy? Seventeen years (and very dry years too!) of planting the seeds, then all at once to have such a wonderful harvest as this. If I had never seen such real results, I knew that the Word of God was being given to them day after day, year after year, and I knew it would spring up sometime, somewhere. But I never dreamed there could be a revival anywhere such as God has given us.[32]

Why did God wait so long to answer Lillian's prayers? To lift her depression? I do not know. He could have met the need early with a minirevival, but He waited.

Lillian, however, remained obedient and trusting, and went about the daily task of begging. Today, in the vast Arab world, America has *one* committed friend: Egypt.

I have wondered if this could be because 8000 children have passed through Lillian's orphanage. Those children have graduated, entered college and professions, married, and become leaders in every stratum of Egyptian society. They remember an "American lady" who rode a donkey and never gave up despite the needs and conditions. She never let criticism of what she *should* be doing interfere with the daily task of loving. She disciplined her depression.

Sources of Depression: Sameness

Jim Lowell is depressed. Jim Lowell is in a rut. A direct tie links the two. Jim allowed himself to become bored in his job, in his marriage, and in his Christian service. Boredom fueled his depression.

Jim lives out a predictable life. Monday night he eats chicken; Tuesday night it's lasagna; Wednesday night it's beef. Even his vegetable choices and bedtimes are predictable. He avoids the risk of trying something he might not like.

Whatever happened to the word *surprise*? The reason we avoid surprises is that we don't want to be disappointed. Jim won't try the new Chinese restaurant two blocks away because he *might* be disappointed. The fear of disappointment squirms into our ambitions, into our dreams. Paul Tournier, a Swiss physician, said, "We think by being cautious that we are protecting life." However, by avoiding risks, he concluded, we "slowly smother life."[33]

New is an infrequent word in the vocabulary of the depressed. So what can you do to add *new* to your life?

1. Anticipate the new.

2. Welcome the new with open arms and a smile. Don't shrug your shoulders and guess that you can survive. It's more probable that you will like it than that you won't.

3. Befriend the new. Look through the Yellow Pages and pick out a restaurant in which you haven't eaten. First, imagine yourself driving there. Imagine entering the parking lot and now walking into the restaurant. Picture yourself ordering off the strange menu.

Picture yourself pushing back from the table and saying, "What a great meal!" Now picture yourself walking out the front door with a big smile on your face, thinking, "I'll be back!"

What keeps you from trying it? The new restaurant could become your favorite!

> **We think that being cautious protects life, but in essence we are slowly smothering life.**

Name Your Culprit:
Deception

The Word encourages us "to speak the truth in love" (Ephesians 4:15). But the agelong question is "What *is* truth?" There seem to be so many competitive, conflicting brands of truth. How is a believer to know?

It's easy to be deceived. When you're wrapped up in the clutches of depression, data become distorted or missed or overdissected. Sally moans, "No one likes me," perhaps to gain attention of affection. Eventually she will believe the charge if she repeats it enough.

When you keep repeating some accusation, you desensitize yourself. At some point Sally concluded, "No one likes me." It may have been after a mild disagreement with a friend, after another slighting in a long string of hurts.

But at some point Sally toyed with the idea and then made room for that negative thought in her mind. As she reexamined old experiences, she chose to see them in such a way as to support her accusation. Through repetition she conned herself into disbelieving the conflicting data (for example, her good friendships with Beth and Lynette).

A description common among the depressed is helplessness: "What can I do?" Maybe you get depressed with the reports of the millions of people starving in Africa. You mumble, "What good would my five dollars do?"

If 100 million Americans believed that their five dollars would make a difference, the combined giving would be one-half *billion* dollars, and that would make a tremendous difference!

What do you hear yourself saying to yourself? Are you

deceiving yourself? Are things really as bad as you think? Have you exaggerated a bit to gain sympathy? Have you chosen to be helpless?

What are you pretending *not* to know? Pretending is one of the most serious deceptions.

If you are "to speak the truth in love" to one another, you must do the same with secret-talk. The testimony of thousands of Christians is that they found the way out of their depression by facing the truth, even if it was unpleasant. Most found their way by saying:

- "I can!"
- "I will!"
- "I am going to!"

Your depression may be dissolved by asking for help. You may have made an inaccurate assessment of the problem or predicament which prompts your depression. Businesses hire thousands of consultants every year. The consultant's task is to analyze the data; maybe the business has made some mistakes. Sometimes a fresh mind brings solutions more quickly. If business can hire consultants, so can you. Counseling is an investment in yourself—a wise investment. Don't let pride keep you from seeking help and taking that advice.

The notion "depression is a sin" is a deception. If you repeat it often enough you will be deceived, and your depression may be deeper and last longer than necessary.

You are neither hopeless or helpless. The Lord wants to help you, and so do a lot of His children. But solutions begin by rooting our deceptive thinking. Solutions begin by rejecting the imposition of standards composed by other people.

Remember, things are never as bad as they seem.

Name Your Culprit: Deprivation

- "Poor me!"
- "All I'm doing without..."
- "If only I had...then I would be _____."

We live in a consumer economy. In 30 seconds an advertiser can convince you that you need product X. He massages your ego by telling you about the wonders that happen to persons who use this particular product. So you need the "new, improved." Or we buy the idea that "bigger is better." We spin in an upward-bound movement, buying this and buying that.

Howard Hughes had more than 99.99 percent of other Americans. He had it all—not just electronic gadgets but airplanes; not just airplanes but his own airline; not just women but Hollywood's most beautiful starlets. Yet he died, depressed and craving just a little bit more.

Bertram Brown of the National Institute of Health complained, "The whole world of communications not only builds up expectations but markets them: *second* cars, *second* houses, boats and foreign travel." However, in third-world nations there may be poverty but there is little frustration, anxiety, tension, and depression that Americans get with unmet expectations.[34]

Millie illustrates this point. She is 35, unmarried, a CPA with a large bank. She has a condo, a new car, beautiful furniture, a stock portfolio...yet she "wants it all," meaning a husband and a family. She feels deprived and depressed. Despite all the material luxuries she has gained, she feels that life has abused her. "If only I were married," she thinks, "then I would be happy."

It's so easy to look around and covet. Oh, we don't always covet houses or wives or manservants or oxen. But we easily covet IRA's and tax shelters and annuities and other economic trinkets of the twentieth century.

In an age that stimulates your wants (and you are still making payments on last year's wants), if your neighbor gets the new and improved or the latest model, it's almost natural that you feel depressed as well as deprived. That's what the manufacturers are counting on. After all, when many people get depressed they head for the nearest mall.

Ads suggest, "Why do without? Why deprive yourself?" Our Puritan forefathers' preoccupation with thrift seems outdated. Yet not only did they practice thrift, but they believed that doing without was actually beneficial.

The gap between what I want and what I can afford is a fertile field for depression. I am more than the trinkets I accumulate. Some of what we label "depression" is more likely *conviction*. The Holy Spirit uses it to gain our attention, to disturb us: While we live in affluence, many of God's people go without the basics.

Missionary Lillian Thrasher was often pitied for all she sacrificed to serve the Lord in Egypt. She responded:

> . . . they don't know what they've missed. A chance to make over broken lives and to build up the most wonderful memories a girl can have of her youth. There was the joy of repairing crushed lives, of loving dying babies back to life, of spending my life for God. No, it was not a lost youth. Never! The memories are golden, priceless and cannot be taken away.[35]

People like Lillian Thrasher, who cling loosely to their possessions, are seldom depressed. They seldom see their loot as a barometer of their worth but as a conduit for ministry.

If you continuously rehearse all you're missing out on,

you will be depressed. The longer you watch the videotapes, the more depressed you will become.

But have you been deprived of water? of air? of clothes? of freedom?

The psalmist said that he had *never* seen the righteous forsaken. Well, God has no intention of starting with you!

> **The gap between what I want and what I can afford is a fertile field for depression.**

Name Your Culprit: Distortion

Two thousand years ago Solomon observed that as a man "thinketh in his heart, so is he" (Proverbs 23:7 KJV). You are what you think.

Dr. William Backus suggests in *Telling Yourself the Truth* that you are depressed because you think depressing thoughts or believe misbeliefs.

> The depressed person believes he or she can never be happy without the thing they now do not possess. . . . nearly all depressed people tell themselves they will always feel devastated and down, *virtually all recover*. . . . Recovery from depression is in fact the most likely outcome. Speak the truth and say, "Even though I feel I have no hope, my recovery is assured. Thank God, these feelings of depression won't last."[36]

Mildred, 68, accompanies her husband twice weekly to the dialysis unit of a hospital. For four hours she waits as his blood is treated. Twice a week, all the way downtown and back. If he is to live, there is no other choice. Yet she spends two days a week depressed.

"Why?" I asked. "Your husband is surviving and getting better. If anyone should be depressed, it's him. He's the one who has to go through the dialysis."

"It's so depressing up there."

"In the treatment center?"

"No, in the waiting room!"

I should have asked, "What are you doing to make it a less depressing place?" I didn't. Mildred is depressed because the technology that prolongs her husband's life obligates both of them to a routine that precludes her plans for his retirement.

"I wanted to travel, but..." her voice trails off. She is angry—angry at her once-workaholic husband who didn't believe in vacations. "When we could have traveled, he worked"—so it's all his fault. But she can't blame a sick man, so she disguises that anger.

Or is it God? I wonder to myself as I listen to her.

"I don't understand it. God could heal my husband. Why hasn't He? He's lived such a good, moral life. Always gave a lot of money (sometimes I thought too much) to the church. Now he just lies there. I don't understand it." She fights back the tears.

How would you counsel Mildred? Can you picture her there in the depressing waiting room? Something will soon have to be done. Her depression and anger are both growing.

If I suggest, "See a counselor," she snaps "What? Out of the question! Besides, that costs money."

In essence, her choices, fueled by the distortion, fuel her depression.

John is just the opposite. He's 34 and single. He moans, "Who would want to marry me?" He's bought the distortion that he has to look like Mr. Macho to attract women. Each morning as he shaves, he rehearses the distortions in the mirror. "You're ugly! You're a slob! No wonder you didn't have a date!"

Let's examine the allegation.

Admittedly John is not handsome from the world's point of view. But he is witty, he has a good job, he is kind, and he is a good listener—qualities that many women appreciate. The real reason he didn't have a date on Friday or Saturday is that he didn't ask anyone. He was hampered by his own fear of rejection.

But he doesn't want to deal with that. Rather than take responsibility, he puts on some critical self-talk tapes and listens.

Your mind will finally begin to believe whatever you tell it. If you repeat the distortion often enough, you'll buy it. The Scriptures warn about "believing a lie and being damned." Well, what is true of eternal life is just as true of emotional life. People choose to cling to distortions, and the distortions keep them from experiencing love and joy.

Mildred and John have both bought a lie: she, that she can't do anything about the depressing waiting room, and he, about this looks. Both are "damned" to misery and a gigantic load of psychological pain and depression.

We must speak the truth in love. This means to yourself, too. Why should you lie to yourself, of all people? Depressed people say things to themselves that they would never accept from others . We have renounced "secret" ways but not secret-talk. If someone could eavesdrop on your inner conversations, what would he overhear?

It's your decision: To beat this depression, you must decide to terminate the distortion, to renouce depressing secret-talk.

Name Your Culprit:
Desertion

Some people have fragile egoes—some by endowment and others by cultivation. They attach a disproportionate barometer to their advice and to their status. If it is accepted and followed, fine. But if their advice is rejected (or in some cases even questioned), they become depressed.

Americans praise upward mobility—that dash up the ladder: We love "rags-to-riches" stories. "Look where he came from!" we applaud the self-made man. We nod at a Mario Cuomo, a second-generation American now Governor of New York. Where but in America is there such opportunity?

Many achievers fear that their mobility could be reversed or might be cyclical, that there is a "reverse gear" that might return them to the "rags" stage. Some families, however, resist and resent the achievements of their children: "He's putting on airs!"

Ahithophel had climbed socially. Because he had the king's ear and confidence, he had status in Jewish society. Yet when Ahithophel realized that his advice had not been followed, he could not handle the rejection and committed suicide.

But there is also anticipatory depression. It begins when we first suspect that we are going to be rejected. This fear leads some people to reject before they are actually rejected. Many people have boasted that they got out of a deal "just in the nick of time."

We cling tightly to relationships, frightened of change. We are like children pleading, "Don't leave me. What would I do without you?" Sometimes we cling so tightly that we strangle the relationship. Ahithophel should be a warning. My value to anyone does not consist of my insight, wisdom, or intellect.

My value does not come in strokes, rewards, or recognition. My value comes in God's affirmation of me.

If people reject me, I still have worth.

If people reject my ideas, I still have worth.

Perhaps you've lost your job, or a significant promotion. Remember, an employer only provides a check and a place to work—*not* your worth. If someone else got the job—even if he or she were less qualified than you—it's unfair, but it's not the end of the world.

If your mate takes a hike with some "sweet thing," it's unfair, but it's not the end of the world.

If your child breaks your heart and gets arrested selling cocaine, it's unfair, but it's not the end of the world.

If you get sick and lose your health, it's unfair, but it's not the end of the world.

Bad things *do* happen to good people. Depression either accompanies or soon follows. But the only real "end of the world" would be for Jesus to say, "Get lost!" And those are two words He will never utter to a believer.

No one can make you feel inferior without your cooperation.

Name Your Culprit:
Despair

Did you ever see the classic film *Gone With the Wind*? That's the mental image that comes to many people when they see the words "Civil War." We think of stately mansions, women in flowing gowns, and slaves.

Initially, many Southerners boldly proclaimed that "by May 1 [1861] the flag of the Confederacy will wave from the dome of the old Capitol in Washington and in a short time over Fanuel Hall in Boston."[37] Some mothers expected their sons to return home in 90 days, having whipped the Yankees "good."

By 1863 both sides had been devastated by the bloody fighting and staggering losses. Confederate General George E. Pickett took time out of the fighting to marry LaSalle Corbelle. It wasn't exactly a "boy-meets-girl" romance; he was a generation older than Sally. His letters reveal his growing despair: "My heart is very, very sad," he wrote in July 1863, "and it seems almost sacrilegious to think of happiness at such a time as this."[38]

At one point two months had passed since he had seen Sally. He wrote, "The disappointment and sorrows that have crowded into this interval make the time seem like years instead of months."

A lot of depressed people can identify with the general's words. How slowly time passes when you're depressed! Yet the general did marry LaSalle, although he had to sneak her through Yankee lines. In the midst of the dispair, a thousand people packed into the church. Sally wrote, "We left for Richmond on the afternoon train amidst the salute of guns, hearty cheers, and chimes and bands and bugles."

Hundreds attended their reception. Because of the shortage of sugar, one recent bride offered the remnants of her own wedding cake. Mrs. Robert E. Lee donated a fruitcake. Southerners put aside their despair and danced "as only Richmond in the Confederacy could dance."

Sally reminded Pickett, "If people could not dance in the crises of life, the tragedy of existence might be even darker than it is." Somehow, for a few hours, the despair was extinguished. A couple's "I do's" called forth joy long suppressed, and dissolved their corporate depression.

The Picketts' life didn't unfold as a fairy tale. They eventually fled to Canada and lived under an assumed name. Federal troops burned the warehouse in which all their wedding presents and valuables were stored. They lost everything but hope!

Today you may be experiencing that "great pressure, far beyond your ability to endure." You may have decided that death would be a relief. Yet I am struck that in the midst of a war, love drew a general to a maid.

God doesn't wear His feelings on His sleeve. He understands the pain that leads us to utter our accusations against Him and against ourselves. Sometimes He cannot eliminate the despair. Rather, He comforts us as we endure the pain.

Your depression and your despair will not last forever. In time the fog will lift.

Name Your Culprit: Defeat

The psalmist in his depression phrased an anguished question: "How long, O Lord? Will you forget me forever? (Can you detect a hint of exaggeration or desperation?) "How long will you hide your face from me?" (Psalm 13:1).

In the agony of fresh defeat, it is easy to be angry, then depressed. Remember USA runner Mary Decker's fall during the Olympic competition? Some of us feel foolish when we trip and fall in front of two or three strangers. How would you feel getting up in front of 60 thousand people in a stadium or 45 million TV viewers?

Mary had trained hard for this race. She had paid a price that most of us would not have paid. Yet in one split second she was defeated.

What about those concession speeches that politicians make? How many candidates ran so close and yet lost? Generally it is the critical after-period that decides their political future rather than the election itself. Some are angry; some are blamers; some become depressed.

If they fight their depression, they can not grow. If they say, "It hurts too much to laugh!" they are on their way to healing and possibly another campaign.

Abraham Lincoln lost his early elections. But he won the crucial election of 1860 and changed history.

The lesson of history and Scripture is found in the Psalms. God does raise the needy from the ashes of their defeat. And He does seat them with princes! He is the God of the second (and third) chance.

Peter Drucker offered four guidelines:

- *Pick* the future as opposed to the past.
- *Focus* on opportunities rather than on problems.
- *Choose* your own direction.
- *Aim* for something that will make a difference.[39]

Drucker should know. As a management specialist he has helped hundreds of companies and thousands of executives escape from the ashes. Whether a bankruptcy, a merger, a forced termination, whatever—he has helped individuals sift through the ashes for that which will nourish the future.

You can choose to lie in the ashes, depressed and defeated. Or you can reach out and take the hand of the Lord, hold tightly, and let Him pull you out!

Those who remember God turn their defeats into triumphs. Join the club—be a winner! Anyone can lie in the ashes. It takes a real winner to get up!

Some people do not have enough to be depressed about. So they borrow tomorrow's troubles.

Name Your Culprit: Disaster

While some people borrow tomorrow's problems, others create anticipatory depression. They use such words as *what if* X, Y, or Z happens (or worse yet, all three). *What if* is a phrase that can either terrorize a person or mobilize him for action.

One vital element in military strategy is *what if* thinking. Military aides in the Pentagon go through mock exercises to test their reactions to "what ifs." They do this to help develop contingency plans and to develop their skills for crisis management.

Do you test your what ifs for accuracy? Do you allow them to taunt you, to nourish your depression? Are you too quick to label things "disasters"?

The Lord says, "Have *no fear* of sudden disaster." None. But all we have to do is watch the news or read the newspaper. Disasters halfway across the world can be watched in the safety of our living room or den within moments of occurrence. We shout, "Hey, come and look at this! Oh, it's awful!" A hundred years ago it might have taken a week to learn of the tragedy.

Perhaps we are more alert to disaster. For example, as more nations gain nuclear power, it's not the madman that frightens me; a silo technician's mistake could be just as deadly.

But it may not be the threat of nuclear attack that frightens you. Maybe it's marital disaster or financial disaster. Maybe it's your own personal disaster that has already happened or almost happened. Maybe someone is about to uncover your secret, and your whole world will come crumbling down.

Many of us have missed the most-feared consequences in our personal disasters. We didn't get what we deserved or feared. Yet our secret is still waiting to be tripped over by the curious. David is deeply depressed by the memories of an affair that ended six years ago. But because he is a pastor, it still depresses him. Recently a fellow pastor was caught and "faced the music," meaning that he lost his church and his credentials. He went from an affluent pastorate to selling insurance, almost overnight. David watched the reaction of his colleagues for a hint of compassion.

David is convinced that his past will catch up with him. I asked David, "Would it be the end of the world?"

"Yes," he mumbled.

"Really? You mean you wouldn't live if that happened? You couldn't breathe?"

"Well, I guess I could breathe. . ."

"Then it wouldn't be the end of the world."

"But of my career, and that's all the same."

"Hardly. It would be unpleasant, but you would survive."

Admittedly David would lose a lot that he has worked hard to gain, but he wouldn't lose his forgiveness. That's unchallengeable. And God certainly wouldn't think any less of him.

Much of our depression about the future, according to psychologist Frank Freed, is because we assume that we are solely responsible for the future. But it is God who holds that future, and He will rescue us in our day of trouble. He will see us through even if our friend or mate deserts us.

NOTHING CAN HAPPEN TO YOU TODAY THAT GOD AND YOU CANNOT HANDLE. It may be unpleasant and embarrassing, but you will survive—if you choose to survive.

Seasons of Depression:
Childhood

Depression is not just a problem for adults. *The American Journal of Orthopsychiatry* confirms that the incidence of depression in children is growing, and now affects thousands of children. Tragically, these are the individuals least able to understand their emotions and moods.

"Previously," psychologist Carl Malmquist observed, "psychoanalytic dogma" discounted childhood depression. Some theorists admitted that children got sad but argued that they did not have the mental ability to suffer full-blown depression."[40]

What are the symptoms?

- Poor appetite.
- Insomnia or hypersomnia.
- Psychomotor agitation or retardation.
- Loss of interest or pleasure in usual activities.
- Loss of energy or fatigue.
- Feelings of worthlessness, self-reproach, and excessive or inappropriate guilt.
- Diminished ability to think or concentrate.
- Recurrent thoughts of death or suicide.[41]

A child could be diagnosed as depressed if he or she exhibits four out of eight symptoms every day for at least two weeks. However, for children under age six, three of the first four would qualify.

Still, Sargeant cautions that temporary interludes of depression are typical for many children.[42]

Moreover, childhood depression often goes undiagnosed because the symptoms are mixed with other behavior: delinquency, school problems, hyperactivity, etc. Because of the stigma attached to mental problems, no parent wants to have his or her child so labeled.

What causes depression among children? Childhood is supposed to be a happy, carefree time.

Loss of love or attention from a key figure in the child's life is a big source. The death of a parent, particularly a mother, or a prolonged absence causes the blues. In other cases, the parent may remain physically present but withdraws from active parenting. In most cases, the depression is only temporary and dissolves when the child receives adequate attention.[43]

However, divorce becomes a significant factor, especially if the child is an object of legal maneuvering. How many children have been objects in legal fights? How many have seen domestic violence as a common event? Consider the fact that 12.5 million children are being reared in one-parent homes. Consider that the average single parent lives on less than 10,000 dollars income yearly!

Researchers conclude, ''We cannot help but speculate that a child's social development would be jeopardized if continually confronted with depressed or distorted maternal behavior.''[44]

In older children, the separation factor can be instrumental or influential. If the father travels a lot, or is separated or divorced, or if a parent rejects the child or depreciates him, depression is likely. One boy disclosed his depression through a picture.

> He drew a picture of a small whale. Then he told how the whale was lost and trying to get home. He tried to hitch a ride with another whale, but slipped off its back. Then he joined a school of whales, but they swam too fast for him to keep up. So the whale in the picture was lying with another whale, also lost, waiting to be found.

Dr. Donald H. McKnew, Jr., a staff member of the Children's Hospital of Washington, D.C., noted, "If an adult told you a story like that, you'd immediately give him antidepressants."[45]

Depressed children become depressed adolescents and depressed adults. Recognition of childhood depression and effective intervention would significantly reduce adult depression and insure a more happy, carefree childhood.

An infant's social development would be jeopardized if continually confronted with depressed mothers or fathers.

Seasons of Depression: Adolescence

Once upon a time, about all a teen had to worry about was acne and "is Shelley going out with me on Friday night?" Today adolescence is a serious time—too serious. Communities are shocked as teens jump off the rollercoaster. Suicide stalks affluent neighborhoods, with suicide now being the third leading cause of death among 15- to 24-year-olds. How is that possible? In a culture that so idolizes youth, teens seem less capable of dealing with their problems. Suicide seems an escape.

Affluence has stimulated this bordom and depression; suicide is rare among the poor and minorities. Trends from New York or Los Angeles hit small-town stores within 30 days. Teens struggle to be "in," whatever the price. Teens with incredible buying power prowl malls, and merchants court their dollars.

Teen sexual experimentation and pregnancy is increasing at an alarming rate. So many kids have been denied so little. Their parents have sacrificed to put polo shirts on their backs and braces on their teeth, and have provided tennis, piano, guitar, and swimming lessons. Some parents have qualified for a chauffeur's license transporting teens from place to place!

One commercial pictures a boy going off to college, grinning. A few weeks later he returns to the same depot, forlorn. He didn't make it, a voice explains, because he didn't have the head start that computer skills could have given him. "Cheap parents" is the implication.

The pressure to "grow-up" or "act your age" leaves some

teens confused. Signs of adolescent depression are somewhat different from those demonstrated by adults:

- Poor schoolwork.
- Rebelliousness.
- Bursts of activities.
- Drug or alcohol abuse.
- Running away.
- Illicit sexual contacts.

Some teens can't cope because their parents—the hard-charging achievers—expect too much or nitpick or force unrealistic expectations on their sons and daughters. Sensitive teens may be devastated by failure. Sometimes a teen's symptoms clear up. Whew! The parent breathes easier now that the storm is over. But this lull may mean that the teen has decided to take the final step: suicide.

How can we prevent teen depression? "Loving, concerned parents," says Dr. Michael Peck, "are probably the best insurance." Yet Dr. Pam Canton, of the American Association of Suicidiology, reminds us that "parents in the United States spend less time with their children than parents of almost any other nation in the world."[46] Thousands of teens feel unworthy and unlovable. Although they have all the trinkets of middle class, they rarely have full access to their parents.[47]

A significant amount of adolescent depression could be reduced or eliminated by parents giving more of themselves. Some parents choose to be "buddies" rather than parents, a decision that further confuses the teen.

Caring individuals outside the immediate family of the teen must also respond. A teen needs listening, caring, and affirming.

Joseph's adolescence must have been depressing—in the prisons of Egypt. But God was with him, and out of prison came the path to the palace.

How many Josephs today are struggling in the pits or the

prison of affluence? How many have removed themselves permanently from the opportunity of future service to God?

The death of *one* teen is excessive. Depression in teens must be taken seriously.

With all the changes of adolescence: chemical, anatomical, and psychological, it is natural that some teens be depressed.

Seasons of Depression: Retirement

"Where has 40 years gone?" my dad wondered as he dressed for work his last morning as an employee of the Louisville Gas and Electric Company. He had won: For 40 years he had climbed electric poles and towers, flirting with high-voltage electricity, and had won. Yet there had been those times when other men, men he liked and supervised, had lost. There were those moments when we at home froze as a news bulletin lacerated our hearts: "An unidentified LG&E employee has been electrocuted and is being rushed to Saints Mary and Elizabeth Hospital. Names are being withheld at this time..."

A hush fell across our house. We waited until the phone rang with either the dreaded news or some other LG&E family wondering what we knew.

Many times the phone rang during a thunderstorm, summoning my dad to go out into the rain to get someone's lights back on. He always went, even when he was tired or sick. If my mother protested, he looked at us and asked, "How would you like to be in the dark?"

Forty years of hail-sleet-snow, and then the calendar said, "Clean out your desk and report to personnel."

So at 3 o'clock the family showed up and drank punch and ate cake at a makeshift office reception and smiled while the vice-president handed my dad his watch. Somehow my dad aged more in those few minutes than he had in a decade. Suddenly he was *retired*. Now, they joked, he could sleep in or go fishing or hunting or...have a heart attack.

Which is exactly what my dad did. One day I found a note

taped on my office door which said, "Your dad's had a heart attack. Call you mother." I did, then hastily drove some 400 miles, hoping I could get there in time.

Before his heart attack my dad had been severely depressed. But his generation of John Wayne look-alikes couldn't admit depression, so they masked their symptoms and had things like ulcers and heart attacks instead.

Why should my dad be depressed? He had no debts, he had a great pension and savings, and he had a big, loving family. But he was no longer needed. A man accustomed to having the phone ring off the wall sat and waited, but it never rang—not even once. There was no "Smitty, what should I do about this?" My dad had a sharp successor who always knew what to do.

The great LG&E could survive without my dad, but my dad couldn't survive without LG&E.

My dad didn't want to be a "senior" citizen but a *productive* citizen. He didn't want to hunt or fish or play shuffleboard—he wanted to be needed, to get folks' lights back on after a thunderstorm. No wonder so many senior citizens have medical problems: No one, sometimes not even their families, needs them. And it's too simple for a doctor to prescribe some pill for them to take, to patronize them while rushing off to the next patient.

We could significantly reduce retirement depression not by installing more shuffleboard courts but by *needing* our senior adults.

Old age isn't so bad—when you think of the alternative.

—**Matthews**

Seasons of Depression: Illness

The classic question is "Which comes first: the chicken or the egg?" That riddle prompts my question: "Which comes first: depression or illness?" Or do they work as a team to gain our attention? Regardless, in the midst of illness, God often has our full attention.

No wonder the woman came to Jesus so meekly: "She had suffered a great deal. . ." but "she had grown worse." That verse might be paraphrased, "She had suffered a great deal under the care of many Christians, but instead of getting better, she grew worse!" Some readers may reject or discount this paraphrase, but many will nod in agreement.

I firmly believe that the church can lessen illness-induced depression. Depression is a natural by-product of our fascination with the notion "If you just had more faith, you wouldn't be sick." Research shows that 83 percent of patients with chronic pain are depressed. No wonder—we want instant cures, shots, pills. Besides, most of us are too busy to be sick.

Some depressed people have been badgered by "You're sick because you—

- Don't have enough faith.
- Have unconfessed sin.
- Have a demon within you.
- Have a rebellious spirit.
- All of the above."

But some of you have faithed and faithed and still aren't

well. As a result, depression rolls in like the thick fogs along the Oregon coastline: thick, moist, impenetrable. Although friends and family may be all around, we can't see them.

Mending can be a good process. The illness and depression can become a "midcourse correction" that adds years to your life.

Paul asked, "Who shall separate us from the love of Christ Jesus?" Well, illness certainly can't, nor can depression. The witness of some chronically ill (many struggling with depression) people is that Jesus *keeps*. His grip is strong.

> **Illness creates depression as quickly as depression creates illness.**

GOAL 4 ❖ DISCIPLING YOUR DEPRESSION

Name Your Fertilizer: Anger

Anger is a dangerous "wild card" in mental health. There are a lot of angry Christians on the loose—not just "righteously indignated," but angry.

Because of our preference for denying our emotions, we have many acceptable synonyms for "anger."

Perhaps as a child you were punished unjustly. That made you angry. Under your breath you may have said a few things. Then your parents asked, "What did you say?"

Wishing to avoid a second whipping, we *denied* our anger. "Nothing," we whimpered.

The Bible does not forbid anger: "Be angry and sin not" (Ephesians 4:26 KJV). But some of us have become so skilled at denying our anger that depression results. In fact, depression thrives on anger. It's like watering grass.

Sometimes we must get angry enough to confront the source of the anger. First we should listen to what we say when we are angry.

"Oh! *He made me so mad!*" That's hardly accurate. It would be accurate to say, "I am so mad at him!" The first way places the responsibility on the other person, who may not have known that he made you angry. Frank Freed says that we often allow total strangers to make us angry. A total stranger can cut in front of us on an interstate highway or a checkout lane and ruin our day.

Anger ignites depression when a person is outraged or frustrated but feels powerless to resolve the problem. "But what can I do...or what can one person do?" That's why a lot of people cheered during the movie *Network*. When the main character stuck his head out the window and screamed, "I am mad...and I am not going to take it anymore!" His listeners rushed to their windows and screamed the same chant.

You have choices: You can give vent to your emotions on a scale that would rival Mount St. Helens. Or you can channel that anger into confrontation and change. You may not be able to change the situation, but you will know that you tried.

There is a time and a place for anger to release the emotional toxins that would otherwise fester and pollute.

You have permission to be angry, but make your anger productive and creative. If you do, you will avoid a common nourisher of depression.

We eventually resemble our resentments!

Name Your Fertilizer: Guilt

A lot of people are convinced that depression is sin. And there is some reason for believing this because depression *can be* a by-product of sin.

But have you ever wondered why God didn't kill Adam and Eve? A small, low-yield nuclear blast would have removed any trace of the Garden of Eden. God could have gone 120 miles down the road and created Eden II. Who would have known?

God would have known.

One friend insists that he would rather have God catch him doing certain things than most of his Christian brothers. "The Lord would be easier on me," he smiles. Many Christians struggle under the burden of their sin because of the abrasiveness of fellow Christians. They have paraphrased Paul:

> If you find your brother in a fault, you who are spiritual, beat the life out of him!

Rather, Paul said, "Be gentle with him, because you aren't above the same temptation." Me? I'd never be tempted to do what he did! But Paul says, "You might."

Guilt is a good response. Yet there are those who have self-appointed themselves spiritual prosecuting attorneys, twentieth-century sheriffs determined to bring their own brand of justice to town, so to speak.

Guilt should be recognized as a loving gift of a gracious God: "He devises ways so that a banished person may not remain estranged from him" (2 Samuel 14:14). That verse should be good news to you.

But there's more:

> The Lord is compassionate and gracious,
>   slow to anger, abounding in love.
> He will not always accuse,
>   nor harbor his anger forever;
> He does not treat us as our sins deserve
>   or repay us according to our iniquities. . . .
> As a father has compassion on his children,
>   so the Lord has compassion on those who fear him.
>
> (Psalm 103:8-10,13)

God always wants to take away our guilt. God is anxious for us to live in a right relationship with Him. When depression is a result of sin, He is more than anxious to eliminate both.

Be sure it is real guilt that you are dealing with—the genuine moving of the Holy Spirit—rather than pseudoguilt. Depression created by pseudoguilt is devastating.

Finally, examine your own life. Remember that being thorough does not eliminate being gentle. Paul said, "Be gentle," and I would add, *with yourself.*

Thank God for your guilt; it makes you deal with sin rather than ignore it. Then, when the particular sin has been confessed, let God take it. He never throws up our past to us: "Oh, yeah, well what about the time you . . ." God doesn't do that.

So, "forgive as the Lord forgave you." That makes sense. But a lot of depressed people refuse to do that. They keep watching the old videotapes.

Just as guilt is a consequence of sin, so depression can be a consequence of an oversensitive conscience. God did not design guilt to trigger depression but to bring you to Him.

Name Your Fertilizer: Indecision

One characteristic of depression is indecisiveness. Which of the following statements characterizes you, *now* as you read?

- I make decisions about as well as ever.
- I try to put off making decisions.
- I have great difficulty making decisions.
- I can't make any decisions anymore.

Think about severely depressed individuals who can't even get out of bed. They don't want to make even the simplest decision. If someone will make their decisions for them, they can survive. They don't want to be held responsible for making the wrong decision. They would rather abdicate their responsibility than be wrong.

Sometimes this tendency has been molded by overperfectionistic parents or mates or even employers. We are so afraid of making the wrong decision that we make no decision.

Jim lost his management position because he couldn't make decisions. Supervisors had initially stepped in to help him or take over for him, but finally there was such a backlog that his management style could not be trusted.

Procrastination is another culprit and complicator. Some people are almost immobilized. Some Christians choose to cloak their indecision with comments about "trying to find God's will." The idea is that if they make the wrong decision, they must forever deal with the dire consequences. It may be a career move, a new job, a new ministry, or even marriage. *Any* decision threatens them.

But when we can't make a decision, the negative self-tapes automatically start playing, and depression soon follows, especially if we lost out on a good thing. For example, Henry had a chance to buy into an oil well. But he dallied with the choice. His wife said, "The money is drawing good interest. Why risk it?" He waited.

The well was a gusher! He would have been rich. No wonder he's depressed!

Sometimes we do not have clear-cut choices between good and evil, black and white. Sometimes it's between bad and worse. But we forget that God has a way of redeeming even our bad choices and decisions.

Today could be a good day to decrease your depression by resolving some conflicts and making some decisions. Remember, not to decide is to decide.

Today is the opportunity to create tomorrow's memory.

Name Your Fertilizer: Resentment

Resentment kills not only fools but sometimes wealthy or highly educated or talented people. I once heard resentment defined as "anger rethought." Monday Night Football wouldn't be half as exciting without instant replay. Yet for years we had to limp along with only our memories of "the great play." Now we can see the touchdown or pass interference immediately.

However, that technology is not new. Deep within our brains we have instant replay. Although it is a God-given ability, as with so many things it is used generally for negative purposes. When someone hurts us, we press the instant replay button: "Poor me."

James Coleman noted that the depressed person—

> becomes very actively involved in fantasies that poignantly depict the now unavailable situation of satisfaction and gratification. Initially very painful, these fantasies, if only by sheer repetition, gradually lose their capacity to evoke pain.

Sullivan calls this process "erasure."[48]

Remember the story about the little boy who brought a bear cub home and kept him in the smokehouse? Each night he fed the bear. Slowly the cub began growing, and soon he was a fully grown grizzly bear that wreaked havoc on the smokehouse.

So it is with resentment and depression! The bigger the resentment grows, the deeper its accompanying depression.

Sometimes, to be good to myself, I must tear up the claim

checks for justice. A decade ago, in a certain Southern state, some godly folks were brutally murdered. The men responsible were caught and brought to trial. However, through legal maneuvers, they escaped the death penalty and got a life sentence. That wasn't enough for the family. They swore that "life sentence" would mean life in prison. The family discovered that through selected financial contributions to political campaigns they could influence the parole process.

Each time the men came up for parole review, the family went into action. Year after year the paroles were denied. But for six weeks before the parole board met, depression flared up in the family as the grisly murders were brought up and relived.

Eventually one family member decided to let go of his resentment. He wrote no more letters and no more checks. His depression evaporated. Why? Because choices have consequences. Certainly he missed his parents, but he found peace by a decision to terminate his resentment.

Resentment is so subtle, so righteous. There are those who would never pet a rattlesnake, yet fail to realize that the venom of resentment is far more deadly.

We fuel our depression by what we resent. The greater the injustice, the greater its capacity to create and maintain depression.

Computers have incredible capacity to store information and to recall it in microseconds. But then so does your mind. Paul Hauck in *Overcoming Depression* wrote:

> You are going to have to learn (if you want to avoid depression) that while you are living on the face of this earth, unfair and unkind behavior in exchange for your loving efforts *is the rule* rather than the exception. The sooner you realize that things will always be that way, the healthier you will become.[49]

Maybe today would be a good day to cancel the lease on some of your resentments.

Name Your Fertilizer: Loneliness

In times of emotional distress, it is easy to exaggerate our problems and to discount our capacity to respond to those problems. Blumberg and Hokanson found that depressed people sometimes turn off potential helpers because they focus only on their problems. "Woe is me" stories turn off many potential helpers.[50] Sometimes a helper must interrupt to ask, "Are things *really* that bad?"

Depression creates loneliness because a lot of people avoid being around depressed people. "It's too depressing!" has become a common excuse. The words imply that there are degrees of depression we can handle or tolerate. Some depressed persons learn to mask their emotions. "Old Harry's the life of the party!" we chuckle. But after the party, Harry is deeply locked in a depressed loneliness. He cries out for help like a dehydrated man crying out for water.

If no one responds and if we repeat the "woe is me" stories to ourselves, we begin to believe the laments. That's why Elijah cried out, "I am the only one left" (1 Kings 19:14).

The Lord wasn't anxious to listen; He quickly responded, "Go back the way you came" (19:15). He ordered Elijah to anoint "Elisha son of Shaphat from Abel Meholah to succeed you" (19:16).

Either this meant that there was at least one other qualified man or that the Lord had lowered the qualifications. However, the Lord went a step further. Gently but effectively He corrected this spiritual Lone Ranger by saying, "Yet I reserve seven thousand in Israel" (19:18). Obviously, Elijah had drastically exaggerated the shortage of saints and servants.

117

Lest we jump to the conclusion "But the new prophets weren't as spiritual as Elijah!" the Lord added, "all whose knees have not bowed down to Baal and all whose mouths have not kissed him" (1 Kings 19:18).

Abraham Lincoln struggled with depression over slavery. Daily as he passed the slave markets in Washington D.C. during his term as congressman, he wondered what he could do. How could slavery be tolerated in the nation's capital?

Lincoln decided that he could introduce a bill calling for the abolition of slavery in the District of Columbia. That would be a good start. The Southerners laughed at him and his fellow Whigs deserted him; his bill failed.

Lincoln could have wallowed in the depression of such legislative defeat. Yet in the aftermath he found the courage that led to his presidency and the Emancipation Proclamation. Within two decades all slaves were free. Lincoln stood at a fork in the road and chose the path that led to action rather than continued depression.

Someone has observed that depression "is a sadness so deep that no one should ever go there alone." That's why the Devil's ultimate joy is hearing "Depression is a sin." He knows that the phrase not only wounds like shrapnel but also keeps Christians from comforting one another. If you are in a car accident, we'll be happy to pray with you or come to your hospital bed. But if you're depressed, well— you can do something about that yourself!

As a result of the believers' inaction, the depression deepens.

Paul knew a lot about depression. He wasn't always singing, "I've got the joy, joy, joy, joy . . ." Paul reminded himself that many believers suffered. This led him to write, "Praise be to the God and Father of our Lord Jesus Christ, the Father of compassion and the God of all comfort, who comforts us in all our troubles" (2 Corinthians 1: 3,4).

Evangelicals have a tendency to stop there and say, "Isn't God good?" But there is no stop sign there—only a comma.

God does not heal or comfort us just so that we will stop pestering Him for healing. Rather, God comforts us "so that we can comfort those in any trouble with the comfort we ourselves have received from God" (1:4).

No one is ever hopelessly depressed in the presence of a friend.

Name Your Fertilizer: Pride

When evangelicals hear the word *idol* they always think of gigantic Buddhas or similar objects of adoration. They never think of *mental* idols. The Caananites needed to be able to see their god, so they dotted the hillsides with Baal statues.

But since that time mankind has become more sophisticated, and rather than have our idol out in the backyard where someone could run over it with a lawnmower or steal it, we construct our idols in safe niches in our minds. We are pleased with so many American cultural virtues that we have made them idols.

The history of mental care in this nation is not good. We once locked away the troubled; we did awful things to them. Some of us may have had disturbed relatives. Our fears and biases have been shaped by what we saw and overheard. Mental illness was something to be kept "in the family." No one else should know. In many families, problems were denied. As a result, the notion developed that we should not admit mental illness of any sort.

In one conservative family, a college-age member became severely depressed. The problem was denied and masked to the breaking point. At Christmastime a family member lovingly intervened and took the depressed person to a Christian psychiatrist.

However, there were no subsequent visits. When the grandparents on one side found out, they had a fit that no doubt qualified them for a session or two with the good doctor. "Only crazy people go to psychiatrists!" they thundered. "And if you're crazy that reflects on us!" Family pride was on the line.

So the psychological help that was needed was ambushed. The family member had to endure more pain than necessary, and the problem has not gone away.

God calls and equips psychiatrists just as He calls ministers. He calls some of His children to be psychologists just as He calls others to be evangelists or missionaries. He calls some of His children to be counselors or therapists just as He calls others to be ministers of youth or music.

Through the power of the Holy Spirit and capable clinical training, He raises up trained people to bring healing to His people. Unfortunately, a few still dare to stand up and arrogantly intimidate those who would use such services.

While I am certain that depression is rarely sin, I am equally certain that the attacks on God's anointed but depressed servants are sin. God will hold us accountable for our accusations against those counselors He has called and equipped. Every word will be accounted for.

God will hold us responsible if we fail to take advantage of the helpers He has provided. God will hold us responsible if we discourage someone from seeking out the helper they need.

For years I was ashamed to admit that I went to a Christian psychologist. In private I thanked God for giving me such a qualified, caring psychologist. But I wouldn't or couldn't say that publicly. After all, I was a Christian writer and speaker. What would people say?

Then one day I wondered how many listeners and readers might have the courage to get help if I admitted that I went. I felt the nudge of God. In that moment, in a church that was negative on counseling, I admitted that I go for counseling. You could feel the "ahs"—not of judgment but of relief. There it was in the open!

In the emotional jungle that you and I live in, it can be just as appropriate to have a family counselor as a family physician. It can be as important to have a counselor or psychologist as a dentist. In fact, if they have to remove my teeth, they can replace them. But they can't replace my brain.

Pride has sentenced many people to deeper depression and psychological pain, and for longer periods, than anyone should have to endure.

You need never feel the slightest embarrassment in going for counseling.

> **You need never feel the slightest embarrassment in going for counseling.**

Name Your Fertilizer: Fatigue

"The early bird gets the worm" is a common motivational saying in America. Workaholics love working and the comment "You're working too hard." They seem to enjoy burning the candle at both ends.

But too many decisions are made by fatigued persons. For example, some historians blame Roosevelt's fatigue for some of the poor decisions he made with the Russians at Yalta—decisions which resulted in the Communist domination of Eastern Europe.

Today there is a growing recognition of burnout. In one study of depressed patients, "increased tiredness" was reported by almost 80 percent of them. In the nondepressed, only 33 percent reported increased fatigue. Depressed people complained that their arms or legs felt heavy and that they had no pep. A few claimed to be too weak to move a muscle.

Which comes first, depression or fatigue? Consider these classifications:

Mildly depressed	A mildly depressed person discovers that he or she tires more easily. Without being depressed, the individual's energy level once seemed almost endless; now a little exertion leads to fatigue.
Moderately depressed	This person is tired when he awakens in the morning, regardless of how many hours he slept.
Severely depressed	The individual explains that he is just too tired to move. Many are immobilized, even for such simple tasks as eating or dressing.

Beck explains the fatigue as *depletion syndrome.* "The patient exhausts his available energy prior to the onset of depression. So the depressed state is like a hibernation, during which the individual gradually builds up a new store of energy."[51]

However, many psychologists reject this explanation because a person may be given sleeping pills or even be hypnotized to sleep, yet still report feeling fatigued.

Fatigue can also be an avoidance mechanism. Ann is married to an energetic husband who makes great demands on her, yet ignores her needs. Since she sees no way to change him or reduce the tension between them, she cops out by being fatigued. She spends long hours in bed. Because the housework does not get done to the husband's expectations, there is more conflict, which leads to more depression.

After the high-pitched, emotional confrontation with Baal's priests, Elijah was exhausted (and useless). Now Jezebel was able to frighten Elijah into fleeing. God's gift to his tired servant was sleep.

In other cases there is fatigue because we cannot sleep. David knew a great deal about depression and insomnia.

> My soul is in anguish. How long, O Lord, how long?...I am worn out from groaning; all night long I flood my bed with weeping and drench my couch with tears (Psalm 6:3,6).

But in a day without sleeping pills, David said confidently, "I will lie down and sleep in peace, for you alone, O Lord, make me dwell in safety" (Psalm 4:8).

When we know we are facing the tough times, we need to be kind to our bodies. If Jesus, David, and Elijah got tired, so can you.

Admitting and anticipating fatigue is a healthy precaution against depression. It's another one of our choices.

Name Your Fertilizer: Self-Pity

Horace Mann was one of America's greatest educators. He believed that everyone should have access to a good education. Yet his great career in education came only after his great loss: the death of his first wife.

He had long been known as a man with a "story or anecdote or saying for every occasion." Yet after the laughter in public came the long periods of depression in private.

For Mann and for you, self-pity involves a choice. Mann deliberately conveyed his self-pity. He gave "the impression that his suffering was so great that it was cruel to share it with others. He believed...he could not survive without an inordinate amount of pity from those nearest him." Initially his friends gave. Then, as one friend confessed, "Mann wrapped himself in a cloak of despair and courted death."

Why was Mann so depressed? He wrote, "The great, I may say, almost *only* object for which I have lived is no more." Five years after his wife's death he wrote, "I never see a grave or hear any mention of a final resting place but that spot where *all* earthly treasures was laid, is present like a reality in my mind." Mann, however brilliant, chose to wallow in self-pity.

Self-pity is always a choice—a choice designed to gain "Oh, you poor thing!" and similar responses. It is a choice that probably will get you excused from responsibilities. Some would say it is the first cousin of laziness.

But Mann, in his depression, raised a question you have no doubt pondered.

"These days of sorrow, these nights of tears and mourning for the purest, loveliest being whose brightness was ever shrouded in mortality, when when will they cease?"

Sound familiar? Mann's lament may be yours too.

Today may be your day to abandon self-pity. It's your decision. No one can make it for you—not a mate, not a counselor, not a psychiatrist. *You* must decide.

Mephibosheth had had it all. He was the grandson of King Saul and the son of the heir apparent. Anything he ordered from room service he got. He survived the death of his grandfather, Saul, and the death of his father, Jonathan. He survived the new king. He survived exile in Lodebar. Then David invited him to live in the palace, promising Mephibosheth a permanent place "at my table."

His farmwork was assigned to Ziba and his 15 sons and 20 servants. All Mephibosheth had to do was show up for meals. Yet he romped in self-pity because "he was crippled in both feet" in a military society that praised human strength and courage.

In 2 Samuel 19 we encounter him as he meets David after Absalom's coup has been squelched. Mephibosheth had sided with Absalom. "He had not taken care of his feet or trimmed his mustache or washed his clothes from the day the king left until the day he returned safely" (19:24). How typical of depression!

Furthermore, he had not supported his benefactor. When David asked why, Mephibosheth responded, "since I your servant am lame" (19:26). How convenient for Mephibosheth to have an excuse!

Has depression become convenient for you? How many times have you excused yourself by saying, "But I your servant am depressed and therefore I . . ."?

Mann's excuse was that his wife had died. What's yours? Self-pity zaps potential, destroys dreams, and hamstrings memories.

Let go of self-pity. You may be stunned to find that you have released your depression as well. Pity is a pushy, selfish houseguest. But if you evict it, you will find room for new and positive influences. You'll find room to grow and room to become the person God longs for you to become.

Name Your Fertilizer: Rumors

The stock market is a fickle place. One rumor is enough to send the Dow-Jones plummeting. I shake my head in wonderment at those who make their living as traders on the stock market.

By the same token, it takes only one good rumor to send some people plummeting into depression. Even though the event may never occur, the anticipation of it is sufficient to evoke depression.

Paul recognized the power of rumor-spreaders who "get into the habit of being idle and going from house to house.... [as] gossips and busybodies, saying things they ought not to" (1 Timothy 5:13). They spread rumors which led to depression among the widows, who already had sufficient reason to be depressed.

Suppose that at coffee break someone shares a tidbit with you. "You aren't going to believe this!" he whispers.

Slowly the gossiper unravels what he heard "from the horse's mouth." The specific rumor is that 35 people are going to be laid off.

"No!" you gasp, immediately recalling your last Visa, Sears, MasterCard, and American Express bills. "What if it's in my department?"

By nightfall you're depressed; your work performance after coffee break is miserable.

Incorrect information can make us particularly vulnerable. We are so anxious to be "in the know" that we expose ourselves needlessly to unfiltered data and then it becomes easy to misapply what we have heard. How many women have found a lump in their breast and before gaining a correct diagnosis become instantly depressed: "It's malignant!" Later came the sweet ecstasy of the doctor's report that it was benign. The needless pain of depression can often be eliminated if we learn to evaluate the circumstances of our lives in the light of accurate information.

The Lord told Jeremiah, "Do not be depressed when rumors are heard in the land." Jeremiah knew that God would give him the courage, the strength, the stamina to endure. If we can remember that, a lot of our superficial depression can be eliminated.

> **It is good to have available for some other emotion the space that fear takes up in our lives.**

Name Your Fertilizer:
Low Self-Esteem

One of the persistent fertilizers for depression is low self-esteem. Although it appears to be a chronic problem in today's world, it is certainly not a new problem. For example, Moses resisted the Lord's nomination to be the spiritual leader of Israel. Instead, Moses nominated his brother. Moses protested, "O Lord, I have never been eloquent, neither in the past nor since you have spoken to your servant. I am slow of speech and tongue" (Exodus 4:10).

It wasn't the Pharaoh trying to put down Moses—it was Moses himself.

Part of our problem is that we live in such an ad-oriented world. TV commercials bring the latest or most improved into our homes and convince us that we cannot live a minute longer without a particular product. "If only you used Brand X, you wouldn't feel depressed." So we rush out the door to purchase it.

But there's another aspect to the problem. The ad agencies find slim models with perfect hair, perfect teeth, and perfect smiles and then promise interaction by men attracted to such models. Then I assume that the opposite sex will show more interest in me because I use this product.

But the main reason we are open to the "new and improved" claims is because the claim of the last product didn't come true.

The more continuously we are exposed to TV, the more we are influenced by the commercials. "Why did you buy product X rather than product Y?" A whole legion of market researchers want to know if the ad campaign was successful.

Commericals play on our inadequacies. Maybe a warning would be in order—CAUTION: THIS COMMERCIAL COULD BE HAZARDOUS TO YOUR MENTAL HEALTH!

Dr. Irwin Ross has explained why people have low self-esteem.[52]

- They look too much to others for love and affection.
- They are perfectionists and expect too much from themselves.
- They have a weak sense of humor.
- They have been scared by past battles and are scared of future battles.
- They are overimpressed with the success of others.

Are any of these valid for you? Answer this statement: I wish my _____ were _____. What is it about your body that you wish you could change? How would you feel if you could change it? Plastic surgeons are doing a booming business these days altering, reducing, enlarging, and enhancing certain body parts and features.

Yet some people have been surprised to find that *after* the surgery they still have strong feelings about a particular body part even though it has been significantly changed.

One step in reducing your depression is to toss aside your negative self-image and all the remodeling you would like to do. Then decide to accept the you that you are.

So what if there is someone who—

- has "whiter, brighter teeth"?
- has "shiny, luxuriant hair"?
- can sing or dance or hit home runs better than you?

No one, *absolutely no one*, exists on this planet who has the unique combination of talents that you have.

- You are distinctive.
- You are special.

131

- You are a one-of-a-kind miracle.
- You were crafted by a God who knew what He was doing.

Who gave Hollywood or Madison Avenue the power over your self-image? You did. Maybe it's time to take back that power. Maybe it's past time to say, "No more. That privilege is revoked."

For a long time I had been depressed over the fact that I was losing my hair, but I am learning that baldness has nothing to do with the texture of my soul. Man looks at the forehead, but God looks at my heart.

So I have to come to terms with this balding process.

You probably have something that bugs or taunts you. Ask yourself, "Is there anything I can do to change the me that I am?" If so, am I willing to pay the price? If not, am I willing to change my attitude?

Sometimes we need to have a long look in the mirror. We need to say to ourselves *in a gentle tone*: "This is me. I am going to be my own friend rather than my own enemy." After all, there are some things you would never say to a friend.

Maybe life would be easier if everyone looked like Hollywood stars. But I am the only me I have, and I need to take good care of me. There is no profit in being depressed because I do not measure up to another person's standard of beauty. I will only be depressed if I am too lazy to tackle the diet or exercise that I need in order to improve the outward me.

Remember, *no one can make you feel inferior without your consent*. Therefore no one can make you feel depressed about your body. Only *you* have that power. Guard it carefully.

Name Your Fertilizer: Machismo

"Real men don't eat quiche." Taking the logic behind that statement one more step, we conclude, "Real men don't get depressed!" How many men have had to mask their depression? Statistics tell us that women are more depressed than men—at least by diagnosis. Yet men drastically outnumber women as alcoholics. While it may not be masculine to be depressed, it is definitely human.

We can't picture John Wayne depressed—or Kojak or Ben Cartright or Matt Dillon or John Walton. The inference is "and neither should you be depressed!"

Many times we have slapped a man's shoulder and said, "Snap out of it!" or "Get hold of yourself!"

So we "take it like a man" and wrap our cars around bridge abutments or blow our brains out. Look at Ernest Hemingway, a man's man. Yet he ended a brilliant writing career with a gun.

When I think of great men I think of Sir Winston Churchill, Prime Minister of England during World War II. It was he who summoned the British to resist Hitler's bombing. One speech he delivered had only four words: "Never. Never. Never!" Then, after a pause, "NEVER!"

Yet Churchill's biographers have reported his bouts with what he termed "the black dog of depression." Churchill said, "I have no desire to quit this world, but thoughts—dark thoughts come into my head." Few of Churchill's friends knew the extent of his pain. After all, the British were known for their "stiff upper lips." "I did my work," Churchill noted. "I sat in the House of Commons, but black depression settled upon me."[53]

Some contemporary religious teachers insist that depression is totally satanic. Yet Scripture teaches clearly that great men of faith have been depressed. If Jeremiah, Jonah, Paul, and Elijah could be depressed, why can't I?

Consider Jesus' depression as He sighed, "O Jerusalem, Jerusalem! . . . How often I have longed to gather your children together, as a hen gathers her chicks under her wings, but you were not willing" (Matthew 23:37). Can you sense the heaviness of his spirit?

- Males get depressed when they continue to work on a job they hate.
- Males get depressed when they see their bodies change.
- Males get depressed when they realize that they cannot accomplish the goals they have set for themselves or that another person set for them.
- Males get depressed when their marriages fail to meet their deepest needs.
- Males get depressed when they realize that their kids see them only as a meal ticket.
- Males get depressed when their buddies move away or die.

The tragedy is not that men get depressed; the tragedy is that they have so few resources to help them *through* their depression. In essence, midlife crisis is an extended period of depression, fortunately now recognized by society. But if men could admit their depression there would be fewer episodes of devastating midlife crises—those episodes where a man throws everything to the wind to recapture his adolescence.

The backlog of depression reaches a point of intolerable burden. Some men flee from it—

- through an affair.
- through the bottle.
- through drugs.
- through a one-car accident.

Yet David found help through his depression. His helper? Jonathan, the son of the source of his depression. Otherwise, the Desert of Ziph did not offer too many diversions to a depressed man on the run.

There is something overwhelming about Jonathan's action and the biblical phrasing, "... *helped him find strength* in God." Perhaps Jonathan doubted his ability to help David. Whatever, the two men together found strength for that moment, that predicament. That's why we are not called to be Lone Rangers. In his most difficult moments, the Lone Ranger could always count on Tonto.

That's why we desperately need male support groups. That's why we must admit depression. Our silence makes the depression of a friend more unbearable.

Jonathan could have sat comfortably in the palace ordering room service. But he *chose* to go to the Desert of Ziph and help his friend.

No man ever stands taller than when he reaches out to help another man through his depression.

An Agenda for the Depressed: Learning

So often Paul's words are reduced to "I have learned...to be content." Carefully read this passage:

> I have worked much harder,
>> been in prison more frequently,
>> been flogged more severely,
>> and been exposed to death again and again.
> Five times I received from the Jews the forty lashes minus one.
> Three times I was beaten with rods,
>> once I was stoned,
>> three times I was shipwrecked.
> I spent a night and a day in the open sea,
> I have been constantly on the move.
> I have been in danger from rivers,
>> ...from bandits,
>> ...from my own countrymen,
>> ...from the Gentiles;
> in danger in the city,
>> ...in the country,
>> ...at sea (2 Corinthians 11:23-26).

Consider what Paul went through. If anyone ever had reason to be depressed, Paul did. But he learned to ignore the fertilizers we discussed: self-pity, loneliness, pride. What was Paul's secret?

Paul learned to be content in every situation. Paul never faced boredom. Whatever the situation, Paul claimed strength through Christ. Look where his emphasis lay: *on Christ*. That statement overwhelmed the Stoics, who believed they could conquer the "whatevers" of life in their own strength. As noted earlier, depressed people may be perfectionists, with a distorted sense of expectations. Too many say:

I *must*. . .
I *should*. . .
I *ought to*. . .
I *have to*. . .

If I can learn what triggers my depression, I can be further up the road. Don Baker, through his bout with depression, learned several life-changing things. One, there are no vacancies in the Godhead. Two, there is a fine line between compulsion and sanctified ambition. Did he learn this insight overnight? No. "It has taken years to discover it, and maintaining a balance is oftentimes like walking a tightrope." But as a result of his prolonged bout with depression, Baker learned to leave the results of his ministry where they belonged—with God. What about you? Can you leave the results with God?

Your depression, although painful, can be a learning lab. Andrew Murray wrote *With Christ in the School of Prayer*. Your theme might be "with Christ in the school of depression." Baker summarized his bout with depression:

A gracious God took His loving hand and placed it on the psyche of a very self-sufficient child, brought him to his knees, and caused him to be totally dependent on His adequacy for the remainder of his lifetime.[54]

The question is: Are you willing to *learn* from your depression?

An Agenda for the Depressed: Meditating

In Split, Yugoslavia, there is a large statue of a folk hero who translated the Roman Catholic mass into the language of the people, this two centuries before Vatican II. Not everyone favored his idea. What would you know of the Bible if it were available only in Hebrew or Greek? How would you learn its treasures?

Not every generation of Christians has been blessed with free access to the Word of God. In certain parts of the world today are individuals who risk their lives to read the Bible. Yet how many Bibles in America are unread? What will God expect from us because we have had such free access to His Word?

The psalmist said that he had hidden God's Word in his heart. What about you? Have you hidden the Word? In my depression the Bible became valuable to me. I tried to read it but often didn't get very far. The words blurred.

Ah, but the Psalms—what a treasury! David became real to me. He became more than a shepherd boy who killed the giant, or the great king, for that matter. I read the words of a wounded man, a man on the run. With a yellow marker I underlined those passages that seemed just for me. Some nights when I couldn't sleep I skimmed through the Psalms, reading the yellow-marked passages over and over. What comfort!

But I also discovered the value of memorizing Scripture. For example, suppose I am sitting in a meeting and sense the "blues" rolling in. In a split second I can call to mind a passage such as Jeremiah 29:11:

> "For I know the plans I have for you," declares the Lord, "Plans to prosper you and not to harm you, plans to give you hope and a future."

Or I can go one step further and monogram the Scripture.

> "For I know the plans I have for Harold," declares the Lord, "Plans to prosper Harold and not to harm him, plans to give Harold hope and a future."

Right in the middle of that meeting I have been able to head off my depression "at the pass." I have been able to keep it from getting a beachhead in my spirit.

Sometimes we don't memorize because we claim we can't remember. Indeed, for some severely depressed people, memorizing may be a problem. I recall one counselee who was in a serious depression. He had not slept in days. When I suggested he go to bed and *try* to get some sleep, he snarled. "Sleep? I can't sleep!" So I took my Bible and marked ten verses I wanted him to read.

"Here," I said; "just read these verses over and over." Then I went to bed. A few minutes later there was a knock on my door. "What is it now?" I asked.

"This is too much for me." I assumed that to be an excuse, but I said, "Okay, just read the first verse over and over." The individual agreed to do so. I fell asleep. The next morning I was startled to awaken to silence. I tiptoed down the hall and found this depressed person sound asleep—not from a sleeping pill but from the soothing, comforting Word of God.

Certainly it is not a sin to be depressed. But if you *continue* to be depressed because you have ignored resources which could have eliminated or reduced your depression—we may question that.

Scripture is a positive antidote to depression. Go to a Christian bookstore and buy an inexpensive Bible. Then, as you read, use a yellow marker to underline those passages that speak to you in your depression. You've seen the red-letter editions with Jesus' words in red. In essence you are making your own "depression" Bible.

When I was depressed I did this. Then, on those nights I couldn't sleep, I read and reread those yellow-marked passages.

Another step is to buy a spiral-bound set of note cards. As you read Scripture, copy onto the cards those verses which comfort you. Then, each day, open the notes to a page that will be a daily reminder. Prop it up on the nightstand, desk, or kitchen counter. Make this spiral your resource. You might even want to record a date on those cards that had special impact on you—for example, that on January 15, Psalm 37:5 became real to you.

Hide the Word in your heart. Then no one or no mood can steal it from you.

Your happiness depends on the accuracy of your thoughts!

An Agenda for the Depressed: Praying

Pray about your depression. The Word says, "Don't be anxious about *anything*." "Anything" covers a lot of territory. So many of us edit our prayers. We perhaps grew up in families where we had to soften up ole Dad or "test the ground" before we asked for something.

"Our Father..." rings a lot of bells and nudges some anxieties. The problem is complicated by formula-praying, as if a magic code exists that brings better results.

"Name-it-and-claim-it" and "positive confession" reduce God to a candy machine: Drop in your request, make a selection, press the button, watch the "blessing" fall, open the chute, and enjoy. But what about those times when you can't even verbalize your request? Sometimes a depressed person can't get further than "Oh, Jesus..."

God knows our hearts and the perimeters of our pain. He listens to the fumbling, the pauses, the sighs, the groans. During one recent election campaign I saw a billboard: "Vote for Stephens—He gets things done!" That logic transferred into the spiritual arena suggests that a "prayer warrior" has more clout with God than you do. But I question that notion.

James said, "The prayer of a righteous man is powerful and effective" (James 5:16), which would tend to support the notion. But look at verse 17: *"Elijah was a man just like us.* Remember that Elijah battled depression and that Elijah, while in utter fatigue, prayed that he might die. Yes, God does hear the prayers of the depressed. The Word says that a depressed man's prayer can be powerful and effective!

Paul, who knew something about depression, urged, "Present your requests to God." Yet we forget that a *no* answer is just as legitimate as a *yes* answer. Paul didn't have a perfect batting average in prayer. Three times he asked the Lord to take away his thorn in the flesh, and three times the Lord refused.

Allen Hadidian summed it well when he said, "Often I must confess that I am more interested in a change of circumstances than I am in experiencing the sufficiency of Christ" in those circumstances.[55]

Sometimes prayer is to be blunt: "Oh Lord, I am angry" (that won't surprise him!) or—

- "I'm disappointed."
- "I'm depressed."
- "I have sinned."

Nothing you can ever say to God will cause His mouth to drop open. God is unshockable. But He longs for His depressed children to say to Him, "Papa God." When Jesus prayed in His agony He prayed "Abba Father" or "Daddy." God longs for us to come to Him as confidently as a small child goes to her earthly father.

In prayer, I can't always trust my memory. To help me I have a prayer book, numbered to correspond to the days of the month. On each page are names that I mention to my Father. On some days I need to see the names to remember that they too have needs and burdens—I have been too preoccupied with mine.

In the midst of the fog of depression, we can make time to pray for others.

God hushes heaven to catch the prayer of the weakest saint. Angels stand in awe whenever a depressed saint prays. When there is nothing that can be said, when we've done all we know to do, when we have said all we know to say, when things seem darkest, we can always pray.

In everything.

An Agenda for the Depressed: Praising

One of the choruses I remember from childhood had the following words:

> Anyone can sing when the sun's shining bright,
> But you need a song in your heart at night!

Roller coasters would not be half as much fun without the dips; the same is true of life. No one—I repeat: *no one*—can live on the peaks all the time.

When I get around some "happy, happy" Christians who seem to have anesthetized themselves against life, I get uncomfortable. God designed us to *face* our conflicts, not to deny them.

What are we to do with the direction "to sing and make music in your heart?" and especially the suggestion "giving thanks to God the Father for everything?"

Everything?

Many people think their spiritual gift is to go around quoting Romans 8:28: "All things work together for good..." (KJV). During my divorce, if one more person had quoted that passage to me, I would have "laid hands" on them. "Good out of divorce?" I demanded. "That's impossible!"

- Good out of the death of a mate? *Impossible!*
- Good out of the loss of a job? *Impossible!*
- Good out of famine? *Impossible!*
- Good out of depression? *Impossible!*

The New International Version is more helpful in translating Romans 8:28: "In all things God works for the good of those who love him."

Maybe that should be in italics: *In all things God works*. In the midst of my depression I need to proclaim, even if in a muted voice, "in all things He works."

I love to play a pipe organ. I like to push the stops that cause the windows to rattle. But sometimes, depending on my mood, I want to play the soft notes.

I think that is the way God views our praise. Sometimes, God knows, the soft and muted sounds are the best we can offer. The enthusiastic and bombastic will come later.

But it's natural that we crave those mountaintop experiences. Indeed, some church services have become that: pumping, pumping the spiritual adrenaline. But we also learn from our stubbed toes. The valley is just as legitimate a Zip Code for the believer.

Just as the Lord was with Joseph in the pit, in the prison, *and* in the palace, so He is with us—at every juncture.

What makes praise possible? Had I lived before Calvary, it would have been more difficult to have praised in the midst of depression. However, *this* side of the resurrection I praise God that Christ sits at the right hand of the Father and understands my depression. He has been touched "by the feelings of our infirmities" and knows how to plead for me.

There, at the Father's right hand, is One who can interpret my pain. Jesus leans forward to encourage me to sing even when "my ambitions, plans, and wishes at His feet in ashes lie." There's more: "I will praise Him, I will praise Him, praise the Lamb for sinners slain." In the midst of depression I can choose to praise Him. In fact, the act of praising may release spiritual adrenaline so that the depression will be terminated or shortened.

I *will* praise Him in my depression. That's a decision too.

An Agenda for the Depressed: Fellowshipping

"Thomas, one of the Twelve, was not with the disciples when Jesus came." In the collective depression after the crucifixion, the disciples fell apart. They had not been praiseworthy.

- Judas betrayed Jesus.
- Peter denied Jesus.

And now Thomas was off doing his own brand of grief. When Jesus appeared to the disciples after the resurrection, Thomas was absent. That reality might have influenced the later declaration, "Forsake not the assembling of yourselves together" (Hebrews 10:25 KJV). Why? In the assembling "we encourage one another." In fact, there is no biblical reference to *saint*, singular. It's always *saints*, plural.

Sainthood can only be found in a community. In your time of depression you need a loving, caring body. You don't need platitudes or patronizing. That's the beauty of the early Christians. According to Acts 4:34, "There were *no* needy person among them." That could be true of the church today.

What prevents it from happening?

Some fellowships cannot accept a depressed person: It contradicts their notions. So they ignore the depressed. Some Christians, anxious not to "offend" their brethren or risk their condemnation, mask their depression. They play a role, convincingly, until they return home.

What if every depressed person were forced to spring up like a jack-in-the-box? Many have been pushed back, time after time: "Stay in your box until you're not depressed!"

The church should be a natural environment in which to confess and confront our depression. It should be natural that the elders help us dissect the sources that fuel our depression and then wait with us for solutions or relief. Oh, but that's time-consuming! Often we're so busy ministering that we don't have time to wait. So we say, "Here, take three Scriptures and go to bed. You'll feel better in the morning."

A church with no depressed people is unnatural. Jesus said, "If I be lifted up . . . I will draw *all* men unto me" (John 12:32 KJV). "All men" includes the depressed.

You need a congregation that will accept you, warts and all, where God's people become Jesus to you in your need, where "Just As I Am" is not only a hymn but reality.

You're not a blemish because you're depressed; you're one of God's children who at this moment has a particular need. Give your church a good chance to help you. Nudge them. But if they continually ignore you, look for another church. Remember to be gracious. Initially they may not understand, but that could be because no one has ever shared what depression *feels* like.

Your courage could open the door for others to receive help. Your risk could open the door for a new avenue of ministry. Your example could help your congregation become a magnet to depressed people, an oasis for those wearied by their struggle to deny or conceal their depression. Derric Johnson observed that the apostle John, from his exile on Patmos, described heaven by saying "no more night," then "no more day." He used negatives. Then he added "no more sea!"

That hardly seems significant—"no more sea"—until you realize that John was incarcerated on an island and that miles of water kept him from those he loved in Ephesus. The sea was an insurmountable barrier to fellowship with his friends. Yet in eternity there would be "no more sea" or any other barriers to fellowship.

Depressed saints need the apostles' teaching, the fellowship, the breaking of the bread, and prayer. And they desperately need each other.

You, through your depression, could make a difference.

No one's arms are too short to reach out to someone in need!

An Agenda for the Depressed: Limiting

You can only take so much. No wonder depressed people moan, "I can't take it anymore!" This phrase, while drastic, is reasonable. There is a threshold in many forms of depression that requires a decision.

- I choose to limit my depression.
- I choose to drift.
- I choose to allow my depression to get worse.

Most of the time we can't take ourselves by the neck and demand, "Snap out of it!" In fact, there are two chairs in the theater of your mind. In one chair sits the *Affirmer*, in the other chair your *Accuser*. At times both speak, trying to outshout the other. Definitely, the Accuser is the more aggressive and often the more persuasive. You'll believe the Accuser before you will the Affirmer.

Dr. Lloyd-Martin Jones, a physician-minister, contends that depression is more common among those who have been brought up in religious homes.

The prodigal son, for example, took a long look at the hog pen, then *decided* that there had to be a better way to live. He chose to abandon his strategy. "I will arise and go to my father." That involved great risk. He had no assurance that his family would accept him. Yet he had to find out.

How can you *limit* your depression? By making decisions.

- Turn down the volume of your Accuser.
- Guarantee equal time to the Affirmer, initially. Then

slowly increase the ratio. For each minute the Accuser gets, give the Affirmer three or four minutes (or more).
- Remember: The Accuser has one goal—to hurt you!
- Surround yourself with Scripture, with good music, with memory seeds.
- Always opt for a time-out.

Beth, for example, uses negative reinforcement. She keeps a list of "to do's" for when depression hits. Formerly she felt too depressed to do anything. Her house was always dirty, which fueled heated exchanges with her husband, which in turn sparked more depression.

Now when she feels the "blues" she reaches for her "hit list."

"That's it!" she snaps. "Which way to the first chore?" If it's the bathroom, she scrubs tiles, works on the curtain mildew, mops, waxes. She says to herself, "Okay, you're depressed. Gotta pay for it!"

However, after that first penalty, her husband actually complimented her on the clean bathroom. A compliment! Slowly she has worked to reverse the habits of depression. Slowly her house has become tolerably clean. But her list has been narrowed down, and a source of tension between herself and her husband has been eliminated. That in turn has eliminated a major source of her depression.

You can choose to limit your depression. Formulate your "hit list" of alternatives to depression.

MY HIT LIST

1. _____

2. _____

3. _____

4. _____

5. _____

6. _____

7. _____

8. _____

9. _____

10. _____

You can cope at the end of your rope!

An Agenda for the Depressed: Focusing

List ten things you don't like about yourself.

1.
2.
3.
4.
5.
6.
7.
8.
9.
10.

That didn't take long, did it? Now list ten things you *like* about yourself.

1.
2.
3.
4.
5.
6.
7.
8.

9.

10.

Having trouble with the second request? Most people can complete the first request in one-third the time it takes to do the second! Why? Because we are too self-critical. Depressed people are extremely good at the first assignment, but some cannot think of even *one* thing that they like about themselves!

Some of us need to "take up for ourselves" once in a while. When one business partner chided his partner, a third partner always defended him. In exasperation the first man said to the third, "You're always taking up for him!"

"That's because you're always accusing him!"

Some of us are quick to take up for another person but reluctant to defend ourselves.

If you want power over yourself, you must understand yourself. Cecil Osborne says that this is an art and has written the book *The Art of Understanding Yourself.* You cannot understand yourself unless you honor yourself as a child of God. It is Satan's role to accuse, but many of us give him a lot of assistance!

Brad complained, "Things are bad."

"Tell me about it." Slowly Brad listed all the tragedies and injustices in his life:

- "My wife's not coming back to me."
- "I sent out 15 resumes for new jobs and did not even get a nibble."
- "My current job is getting worse."
- "I'm broke!"

"Well," replied the counselor. "You're accurate. Things are not going well. But let's look at the possibilities."

The client was most uncooperative. He wanted to rehearse the wrongs and have the counselor focus on his problems.

One week later, however, Brad was bubbly: He had had a good nibble for a job with a 5000-dollar-a-year raise!

Three weeks later he had the job.

Brad had faced a crisis. On a resume he looked like the right person for the position. But what about the interview? After so much depression he could never psych himself up for a favorable interview. So his counselor helped him to concentrate on his strengths and downplay the negatives.

As a result, Brad focused on an impressive list of strengths, some of which he had never recognized in himself.

That inventory proved profitable—not just at the next interview but at several in the subsequent years. There were more promotions. Now Brad regularly helps other depressed people inventory their strengths.

But what about the negatives? Honestly confront them. Ask yourself:

- Can I change them?
- If I can, am I willing to pay the price?
- If I cannot, am I willing to change my attitude?

You will discover that as you face and work on these negatives, most will lose their potency.

An Agenda for the Depressed: Punting

Ollie and Ivan Smith had been married for 52 years, had raised 11 children, and were grandparents to a slew of us. My grandfather wasn't a candidate for sainthood, but he was a loving grandfather who bought candy bars by the box rather than one or two at a time. That was my first criterion of success.

My grandparents were Indiana farmers who worked long and hard hours. But when Granddad got sick, they did an awful thing to him: The doctors amputated his leg. After that his life went downhill emotionally. He walked through the dark pastureland of depression. He had spent his life in the barns and in the fields—not sitting around the farmhouse.

Now he had no choice. So he died.

Then, on a hot September afternoon, the family assembled in a small country church for the funeral. The preacher preached a spellbinding sermon, and then we went to Uncle Hugh's and ate the barbecue which had been prepared by the ladies of the church. After that we went home. Grandma handled it well, everyone agreed.

An uncle and aunt had been scheduled to go to Oklahoma for a vacation. My grandmother announced that she thought she would ride along. So she put herself in the front seat and off they went. My aunt later chuckled, "She traveled like a real trouper."

I had problems though. "Grandmother, you're supposed to be grieving!" And she was, in her own way. But at this point she chose to punt. She had had all she could handle.

After nursing Granddad for so long and seeing her Prince Charming deteriorate, she needed some new scenery.

Ultimately she came back home to Indiana and watched an auctioneer sell off the cattle and equipment. Then she moved into a small house in town. "Less to take care of."

I understand the process better now. Sometimes, in the canyons of our heart, we must confess, "I just can't take anymore!" We punt, hoping that tomorrow will give us another chance and better field advantage.

Amazingly, after a good night's sleep, a change of scenery, a good meal, or a trip to Oklahoma, we can return to the job of grieving or facing the other unpleasant tasks that life sometimes assigns us.

Punting is an emotional circuit-breaker for those moments when depression threatens to overwhelm us.

The Costs of Depression: Financial

It costs money to be depressed. In fact, the depression affects both sides of the ledger: income and expenditures. That often leads to further depression.

Ralph, a 52-year-old pharmaceutical salesman, is depressed. His depression was initially mild. Then came a sales slump. Ralph worked extra hard to satisfy the skeptical new sales manager, always sweating for the big sale, but nothing much was accomplished. Furthermore, Ralph's family has lived well beyond their means. His job requires him to be on the road, so he has compensated with material things.

But this has brought more pressure, and the pressure has led to a selling slump. Ralph hates the sight of another motel, yet in a sense he welcomes drawing the drapes and converting the room into a cave. Oh, sure, he listens to the pep talks and has heard all the great motivational speakers, but his depression still dominates him. Some mornings it is all he can do to dress and go to his first appointment.

After work Ralph is ready for a drink. His drinking has increased as his depression has.

Depression can be financially disastrous for those who rely on commissions. Many depressed people go to their jobs like robots, relying on either routine or fellow employees to cover for them. But this also leads to industrial accidents.

Doctors, psychologists, medications, and hospitalization can be expensive too. This drains off money needed elsewhere, or so the depressed person reasons. If a mate is not sympathetic, the cost of treatment can be a weapon wielded in an argument.

But remember: Counseling is an investment in yourself. Spend whatever you must in order to get competent help.

You may also need to evaluate your lifestyle. Money talks; what does it say about you? Do you use money to prove your love to your family? Can you afford to spend money as you do?

I remember a sign:

IF A MAN'S INCOME DOES NOT
KEEP UP WITH HIS OUTGO
HIS UPKEEP WILL LEAD TO HIS DOWNFALL

That's one reason why depression is more common among the middle class: They see everything the wealthy have and want it. So they mortgage their lives and emotions.

It's so tempting for depressed people to use credit cards as an anesthetic. When you feel a little blue, just reach for the plastic rather than for a pill. Head to the nearest mall. *Mallitis* fuels a lot of depression. It offers the momentary thrill of the new. But those highs become lows when the bill comes. And it may mean further conflict with a mate and thus more depression.

Spending is a poor remedy.

It takes time to wean yourself from the plastic pleasures of self-gratification. I call these "winds" of depression that come the first of the month. Just the service charges or interest can be horrendous.

I have chosen to wean myself from the cards, from the buying buzz. Now it is either cash or wait.

Wait? Yes, sometimes by waiting I have found something I liked better or was a better buy.

By eliminating that sword of Damocles that hung over my head each month, I can be more spontaneous in my buying and in my giving.

Choices. I choose to discipline the urge to reach for the credit card.

I choose to remember that "instant" credit means delayed depression.

I choose to remember that I can give *myself* rather than *things* to those I love.

I choose to avoid depression over money. I don't have as much as I want, but I have more than some people. Therefore I can be undepressed as long as I am unimpressed with money.

The Costs of Depression: Spiritual

Happy, happy, happy Christians—the kind who are happy when their puppy gets run over—never seem to deal with depression. In fact, just a few years ago one prominent psychologist lamented the poor witness that depressed people offer to the world.

Well, a lot has changed. Society has a strong influence on Christians. The cost of some spiritual depression is, to say the least, a confused witness. Christians—

> should represent Him and His cause, His message and His power in such a way that men and women, far from being antagonized, will be drawn and attracted as they observe us, whatever our circumstances or condition. We must so live that they will be compelled to say: Would to God I could be like that, would to God I could live in this world and go through this church as that person does. Obviously, if we cast ourselves down we are never going to be able to function in that way.[56]

However, we need not walk around with a perpetual smile either. In fact, many of God's choicest saints have walked a narrow line between self-examination and introspection. Everyone needs to examine himself. One great philosopher said, "Know thyself." Yet how do we keep in focus? We become depressed when—

> we do nothing but examine ourselves, and when such self-examination becomes the main and chief end in our life. If we are always talking to people about ourselves and our troubles, and if we are forever going to them with that kind

of frown upon our face and saying: "I am in great difficulty"—it probably means that we are all the time centered upon ourselves.[57]

It might be helpful to consider David Brainerd, missionary to the Indians who battled severe low self-esteem and depression. Listen to his writing on himself:

> I had the most abrasing thoughts of myself I think that ever I had. I thought myself the worst wretch that had ever lived: It hurt me and pained my very heart that anyone should show me any respect. Alas, I thought: How sadly they are deceived in me. How miserably would they be disappointed if they knew my insides. . . . My soul was grieved for the congregation that they should sit there and hear such a dead dog as I preach.[58]

Later he added:

> My heart was overwhelmed within me. I verily thought I was the meanest, vilest, most helpless, guilty, ignorant, benighted creature living. . . . Sometimes I was assaulted with damning doubts and fears whether it was possible for such a wretch as I to be in a state of grace.[59]

He scribbled, "Oh, how I longed that some dear Christian knew of my distress!"

Clearly he was a depressed man. Yet his diary, edited after his death by firebrand preacher Jonathan Edwards, became a best-seller. In 1799 a young Oxford don, Henry Martyn, read the book and abandoned his academic career. He left Oxford for India, where he translated the Scriptures into Hindu, Persian, and Arabic—translations still in use today.

Brainerd died at age 30, Henry Martyn at 29. However, Martyn's book *Memoirs* also became a best-seller and stimulated many people to missionary careers.

God uses depressed people. Who knows how many lives were touched by these two depressed but devoted servants of God? God can use anything for His glory—even depression.

The Costs of Depression: Social

Depression is a rapidly escalating social problem. There is a continuing stigma attached to mental illness. "Normal people" view the mentally ill as distinctly different. Five hundred years ago individuals labeled "mad" were loaded onto "ships of fools" and sent away as castaways. Some were abandoned at sea; others were refused landing in various ports. Authorities reasoned that by so acting they "were only protecting society from the inconvenience and supposed danger of its erratic members."[60]

America had lunatic asylums and facilities for the criminally insane. Superintendents of such institutions ruled as benign despots, with absolute authority over their patients.

Only through the efforts of a single woman, Dorothea Dix, did the situation change. Miss Dix went from state to state examining the treatment of the insane and mentally ill. She mobilized public opinion to more humane treatment.

However, after the Civil War, state legislatures began cutting funds to such institutions. Many were turned into purely custodial facilities to warehouse the mentally ill. Treatment included harsh and mechanical discipline, such as straitjackets and chains.

Consider the escalating dollar costs of mental health care:

1950	1.7 billion
1974	14 billion
1979	16 billion

Many of the depressed are now treated as outpatients.

Others find themselves either in a psychological ghetto or in some limbo where no one has authority to help them. A University of Michigan study revealed that between 1957 and 1976 a significant increase of psychiatric care occurred for middle- and lower-income families. This was facilitated by expanded insurance coverage and community mental health programs.

Yet with budgets being scrutinized, mental health is often an area for cuts when the budget must be balanced. As a result, some analysts fear that more drugs will be routinely substituted for rehabilitational and recreational activities.[61]

Two tasks remain. The first is to help more people get the care they need. An estimated 7 to 15 million people need help. Yet the neediest may resist treatment because they are prey to old superstitions. "The idea of any medical malfunction inspires in them nameless dread. So they push it aside, refusing to recognize the damage it is doing to their lives and the lives of those close to them."[62]

What about the mental patient who is not wanted? Some could survive without hospitalization if they had someone to care for them or supervise them. Scheffler noted, "Those persons whose stability is most fragile are often the most isolated.Thus the church could provide a shelter 'to bind together the excluded.' "[63]

Such actions would be valuable in reducing the cost of health care. Bertram Brown, Director of the National Institute of Mental Health, estimated that 600 to 700 thousand depressives take up 5 percent of our total national health bill. And this does not include the *hidden* costs of depression. Thousands of depressed individuals are treated by private physicians and are not included in the surveys. Forty percent of visits to general practitioners are linked to psychiatric needs.[64]

Such a program would have an influence on the high rate of alcoholism. Forty percent of America's 8 million alcoholics are clinically depressed. But the stigma of "alcoholic" is not as harsh as that of "crazy." If one considers the number of people killed in automobile accidents by alcoholics, the problem becomes frightening.[65]

Depression also takes a severe social toll on families. Alcoholism and depression are critical factors in marital tension and divorce as well as in family violence. And the children of depressed parents are more likely to be depressed themselves.

It is easy to talk about saving the family, but it must be more than rhetoric; it must include bold new thinking and commitment.

GOAL 5 ❖ BEFRIENDING YOUR DEPRESSION

Choosing To Be Depressed

A person rarely drowns by falling into a river or lake; he drowns by remaining there. Perhaps you heard about the two frogs that fell into a milk churn. The first drowned. The second began swimming so rapidly that he churned the milk into butter, then hopped out.

I've never heard anyone say, "I wish I could be depressed" or "I like being depressed." Rather, most people desperately want to escape the tight clutches of depression. Yet it is generally easier to be depressed or to remain depressed than to work on the factors that triggered the depression.

Backus and Chapian point out the common misbeliefs on self-control. They say clearly, *"I am accountable for my choices."* They offer three realities:

- *Admit* that you make your own choices.
- *Remind* yourself that you are responsible for what you are doing.
- *Prepare* to accept the consequences of your behavior, even if unpleasant.[66]

Logically, it would be inconsistent to complain about depression and ignore the choice I made which created or encouraged the depression.

165

- You can choose not to allow other people to depress you!
- You can choose not to allow other standards to control you!
- You can choose to reject perfectionistic demands!
- You can choose to retrain your mind!
- You can choose!

Celebrate the first steps toward health.

Choosing Not To Be Depressed

We take Thomas Alva Edison for granted. Without his great inventions, how dull life would be!

Edison's life was marked by choices. When other men gave up or abandoned a project, Edison stayed with it. When other men called it a night, Edison remained, tinkering, hoping.

Edison's labs caught fire. Assistants wakened the inventor, then in his sixties, aware that the labs were underinsured. Mr. Edison dressed quickly, went out into the cold, and watched the fire.

"Go wake Mama!" he ordered. "I want her to see these gorgeous colors."

"Mr. Edison," the aides persisted. "You don't understand. Everything you own is going up in smoke."

"Oh, no!" Edison laughed. "Only my mistakes." Other men would have been depressed, but not Edison. In fact, some of his greatest inventions came *after* the fire.

You may be watching your life, your job, your marriage, your security go up in smoke. But that's still no reason to be depressed. Paul had good reason to be depressed, yet he confidently said, *"But one thing I do*: Forgetting what is behind and straining toward what is ahead, I press on toward the goal to win the prize" (Philippians 3:13,14).

All three time elements are there: past, present, and future.

- *Forgetting* what is behind (the past).
- *Straining* toward what is ahead (the present).
- *Pressing* toward the goal to win the prize (the future).

Ask yourself in this particular situation or circumstance:

- Am I choosing to forget? To strain? To press on?
- What would Mr. Edison do in my shoes?
- What would Paul do?
- What would Jesus do?
- What am I going to do?

Phillips Brooks wrote, "You must learn—you must let God teach you, that the only way to get rid of your past is to get a future out of it.[67]

Other people might choose to be depressed. But you? You can choose to limit and to discipline this latest bout of depression.

You must let God teach you that the only way to get rid of your past is to let God get a future out of it.

—Phillips Brooks

What a Difference
Exercise Makes!

Barbara Holland quipped, "Nobody suffers from depression while rowing a lifeboat in a tempest or throwing the family silver out the window while their house burns down."[68]

Exercise is a good alternative to depression. In fact, exercise is an effective choice to avoid depression.

I try to get to the health club every day I am home. I lift weights, ride a stationary bike, and work out on the machines. Sweat clears out the cobwebs of depression and makes the rest of the day different.

Fitness is in. Even small hamlets have health salons or fitness clubs. The solution to some of your depression may be merely a membership away.

Why is exercise so healthful? Well, God meant us to sweat. Take Paul. He could have said that physical training is of some value because he *walked* everywhere. We ride in temperature-controlled comfort. We don't even get the exercise of raising or lowering the garage door. Instead, we press a button and watch it happen. One friend broke me of my habit of fussing over parking spaces. He patted my stomach and grinned, "You need the exercise."

Too many of us live sedentary lives. Our bodies, however, were designed to work. Michael Sachs of the University of Quebec explains that as we exercise, endorphins are released into our bloodstream. These substances are opiate-like and quietly produce effects similar to those of morphine.

John Griest at the University of Wisconsin tested three depressed groups. One group exercised. One group went through meditation. The third group participated in group therapy. At the end of 12 weeks there were "no *significant* differences" among the participants in the three groups. All three groups had improved.

Six months later, however, Griest discovered that the meditation and exercise groups had increased or maintained their improvement. The group in counseling regressed.[69]

Another researcher in 1980 monitored two groups of depressed persons. Group A went through eight weeks of running therapy and varying amounts of counseling. Group B merely went to counseling. At the end of the experiment, Group A scored in the "normal" range of depression. The members of Group B were still depressed.[70]

Exercise is valuable. You may not have the form or style of an Olympic athlete. You may have to endure some mild-mannered teasing. But exercise could be just the thing to burn off the fog of depression.

You don't have to spend a lot of money. Jogging or swimming is excellent. Walking may be even better. Any exercise that increases the endurance of your cardiovascular and pulmonary system is valuable. It goes without saying that you should *first* consult with your physician.

What a Difference
a Mate Makes!

Half the solution to depression is having a mate who understands! On the other hand, a great deal of marital tension and depression is fueled by mates who *don't* understand. Amos said, "Woe to a man who falls" and has no one to help him. The same is true of depression.

Betty stood at my book table recently, softly wiping away her tears. "I still don't understand why he did it. I thought he was getting better. Then he shot himself."

Betty's legacy and depression is wracked by the suspicion that she could have done something to prevent her husband's suicide. She has continuously replayed the tapes looking for her failure. She has run through a string of "if only's."

There's little chance that she will remarry. Her self-tape taunts, "Well, if you weren't a good enough wife for him, how can you help someone else?"

Depression frightens mates. "I don't like it when you're *this* way." So the mate disguises his true feelings. Culturally the husband has to be strong. It's the role he has to play even if he isn't strong.

This fuels the depression in midlife crisis for men. Suddenly the man faces depression, but he has had so little practical experience with depression. Men aren't *supposed* to get depressed, but he *is* depressed. He knows this, and he panics.

Another element is postgoal depression. Suppose a couple wants a bigger house in a nicer neighborhood. They dream, they scrimp, they save, they shop, and at last they have their dream house. They move in. Then the blues hit because the realities hit.

In some couples it is the desire for a child, or a car, or a dream trip. One friend talked her husband into a trip to Hawaii. It rained the entire time. It wouldn't have been so bad if he had not insisted on saying, "I told you so!" once too often. The entire memory is tainted.

That's why dreams must be dually unwritten. When someone imposes his own dream on another person's dream turf, it leads to depression.

A mate who offers conditional love feeds depression. "I love you *when* you. . ." But what about the other times? Many wives of automobile assemblers or steelworkers went through this. The men had good jobs and made big bucks. Then came the layoffs. Some wives were in love with their husbands' paychecks, and now there were no paychecks. Many steelworkers became depressed or began drinking heavily.

Second, mates can short-circuit depression by listening and holding and simply being there. Sometimes marital "shorthand" leads to erroneous conclusions and assumptions.

When mates have to filter things, they feel depressed. A significant amount of adultery begins as emotional attraction or emotional unfaithfulness. Adultery often begins with the ears.

Third, mates who are open to change short-circuit depression. "He won't change—never! I know him!" Some couples get locked into predictable role patterns and habits: If it's Tuesday night it will be country-fried steak; Thursday night it must be lasagna. When one mate feels that a situation is changeless, yet desires change, it leads to a hopelessness that encourages depression.

Change is a major part of every good marriage. Boredom and predictability will send you to a divorce court or to a doctor.

Fourth, marriage and family counseling short-circuits depression. God wants you to have a good marriage. He

172

expects you to do everything you can not only to make it survive but to *thrive!* Today there are incredible resources available to help you. When you do everything you can do to nourish your mate, you eliminate many seeds of depression.

Jean's depression deepened because her husband couldn't handle it. If he had been tolerant it might have passed. But as he became more rigid in his expectations, more demanding, more cynical, they stopped talking. She retreated further into her cave.

Only after her breakdown did he go for counseling. Part of his problem was a fear influenced by his mother's depression—a depression he had hidden from his wife. He had seen his parents fight in their home, and he was too threatened to respond to Jean's needs.

Yet many husbands have testified, "I never would have made it without my wife. She pulled me through!"

Sometimes helping means just being there. Holding them. Whispering their name. Reassuring them that you aren't going to desert them in their blues.

What a Difference
a Diet Makes!

In the last five years, two diseases affecting weight have gained public attention: bulimia (overeating) and anorexia nervosa (undereating). Primarily these affect women and young girls. The diseases are thought to be more common among middle-class and affluent populations.[71]

The anorexic person has a profound fear of gaining weight. She says, "I am powerful enough to control basic appetites." She reasons, "I must look thin!"

Excessive eating depresses people. The *Los Angeles Times* ran this confession by a woman: "I had a love affair with food—and it nearly killed me." She continued:

> Just one helping of my favorite wasn't enough. Instead, I ate all the spaghetti, a whole loaf of bread and the whole bag of candy. I weighed 262 pounds and I hated myself. My binges didn't stop until the day I got so depressed I thought about killing myself.[72]

Fortunately this lady enrolled in the weight program at San Pedro Peninsula Hospital.

Her testimony is that of many people, some from families that urge, "Eat! Eat!" but don't understand the depression that follows.

Look at the cycle:

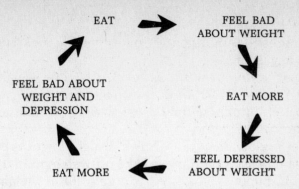

EAT → FEEL BAD ABOUT WEIGHT → EAT MORE → FEEL DEPRESSED ABOUT WEIGHT → EAT MORE → FEEL BAD ABOUT WEIGHT AND DEPRESSION → EAT

We live in a thin-oriented society. Everyone is trying to squeeze into designer jeans. Some people live on a continuous diet or series of diets. Everything is off-limits. If they lose weight they gain it back, and with the most recent pounds comes more depression. "I can't lose weight but I can be fat and sassy!" lamented one lady.

Even as some of us are predisposed to depression, some of us are predisposed to obesity. Unfortunately, a few are predisposed to both. All the books, lectures, and tapes on will-power will not change that. And what about those friends who can eat anything and never gain a pound? Now that's depressing!

My good friend Charlie Shedd insists that there will be no calories in heaven. So he has invited me to spend the first thousand years with him eating desserts!

But some fat people fear being thin, because with thinness comes sexual attraction and temptation. "Oh, my husband likes me the way I am," explains one overweight wife.

"Really?"

Linda, overweight by 50 pounds, was depressed because the guys wouldn't ask her out. So she lost the weight, only to discover that men still didn't ask her out. So she gained back the weight.

Some people become hard to live with and depressed when on a diet. Their diet must be endured by friends and family.

However, you may be one of those persons who will never

kick depression until you get on a sensible diet. Here are some suggestions.

1. Quit saying "can't," as in "I can't lose weight." In *Telling Yourself the Truth* Backus maintains that "can't" is a misbelief. "I choose not to lose weight" would be more accurate.

2. Set reasonable goals. Drastic weight losses are tough because it takes more time to take off weight than it did to put it on. Suppose you need to lose a lot of weight. The sensible way is to set a reasonable time period and avoid fad diets. Set plateaus or stages. Lose, then maintain. Then begin another diet.

3. Plan for "backsliding," but not binges. Suppose you're at a dinner party. It's time for dessert. Here comes the waiter or hostess with the dessert tray. Refuse dessert. Will he say, "Okay"? No way. The waiter gets a commission off the dessert tray, and a hostess has her pride on the line.

Instead, say: "I choose not to have dessert!"

For this to be effective, you will have to rehearse the line, perhaps several times. And you'll have to anticipate a protest.

- "Oh, just a small piece!"
  to which you respond, "It does look good. But I *choose* not to have dessert."
- "But I made it just for you!"
  to which you respond, "Well, I appreciate that. But I *choose* not to have dessert."
- "But everyone is having dessert!"
  to which you respond, "I *choose* not to."

4. Thank God that you have the privilege to live in a country where you have the opportunity to be over-weight. Now ask God to help you eat responsibly. If you make a drastic goal of "No desserts for six months" you're setting yourself up for a binge. You're going to slip, and then you'll likely say, "Well, since I'm off my diet anyway,

I might as well..." Then you'll be depressed.

5. Know exactly what you want. Our problem is compounded by choices. Sometimes we're not sure what we want, so we overwhelm our tastebuds: sweet, sour, crunchy, chewy. But your body knows. Listen to it! Choose one item and have a moderate portion of it. Eat slowly and enjoy!

6. Try to limit your calorie intake. Munch veggies instead of cashews. To avoid eating junk food, don't buy it. Eliminate snacking while watching TV. Look around your church. Do you have more than your fair share of overweight people? Do all of the after-church fellowship times involve food?

Look in the mirror honestly. If you have a weight problem, and that weight problem fuels your depression, you have to make some choices.

When you stare in the mirror, be gentle. Give yourself time. And applaud those "I choose not to's." Soon you'll find the depression decreasing and your willpower increasing.

What a Difference Candlelight Makes!

I've always been interested in pictures of frontier life. You know, the ones where the family is gathered around the hearth, bathed in firelight and candleglow. That wasn't as real to life as we assume. Pioneers were rather stingy with both candles and logs, because candles had to be made and firewood had to be chopped. Families went to bed early.

For several years I have sent candlesticks as gifts to newlyweds. I have included a brief note: "Things always look better in candlelight."

Jim and Judy are friends of mine. Several years ago "the lights went out" in their lives when doctors discovered that Jim had cancer. Throughout their marriage the china and silver had remained in the china hutch, as china tends to do.

During his recovery, Judy brought out the candlesticks and china three nights a week. Whether lasagna or chili, it was served in candlelight.

Now that Jim has completely recovered, they still eat three nights a week by candlelight.

Many couples, bogged down in tension, have forgotten that candlelight adds a touch of romance. We've become too accustomed to bright lights. In fact, midwives are lobbying for softer lights in hospital delivery rooms. It would be less shocking for the baby as he is born.

Don't think of candles as a luxury. Some of our most deeply reflective moments are in soft light: around a campfire, in front of a fireplace, at sunrise or sunset.

One of my warmest memories is Christmas Eve in Camden, South Carolina. At a midnight service, ushers distributed candles. At midnight we walked outside into the historic courtyard and formed a great circle. In the crisp December air we sang "Silent Night." Slowly the ring of candles was lit just as the bells chimed midnight.

Candles also soften and heal and encourage.

Ironically, depression lessens in the dim light of candles. What a difference a candle can make!

What a Difference a Compliment Makes!

"You scratch my back, I'll scratch yours!" What a common cliche in our world! "You give to get" is another way of saying the same thing.

Josh McDowell has identified two categories of people: the *givers* and the *takers*. There are people who *give* compliments and people who *take* compliments. There is an art in either giving or receiving compliments.

We need to give more compliments. "Oh, I'm too depressed!" Too depressed to recognize an achievement? A job well done? A beautiful meal? An attractive sport coat? A thoughtful gesture?

The subtle temptation during depression is to overfocus on *my* needs. I don't give compliments because I don't receive them, and I am too caught up in my own feelings to notice anyone around me.

Admittedly, some of us grew up in families that carefully rationed compliments, fearing "it will go to their head!" Few of us learned the art of complimenting.

- *Recognizing*: The item or action to be praised. A compliment says a great deal about what you value. Some people praise things; other people praise people.
- *Phrasing*: How should I compliment? When should I? Perhaps you've had a compliment or your motivations misunderstood. As a result you've been stingy with compliments.
- *Reinforcing*: An effective compliment is punctuated

with a smile or a touch, whatever seems appropriate. Since so many people regularly discount or discard compliments, the smile says, "I really mean that."

Compliments do not have to be gushy or cute. Some of the best are simple recognitions of graciousness. People do not like to be taken for granted.

Today, set a number of compliments you wish to give. Let's say three. They don't have to be rehearsed. Compliment small things. Gradually, with practice, you'll be stunned by the change in your mood.

But this also means *accepting* compliments. Don't reject them. Listen. Accept. Enjoy. Someone once asked Corrie ten Boom how she handled her compliments. She said, "I gather them up and then at the end of the day shape them into a bouquet which I give to Jesus."

Compliments, like boomerangs, have a way of coming back to you. In fact, your compliment may burst the bubble of hidden depression in another person.

What a Difference
a Song Makes!

The Jews found themselves in cruel captivity. Their captors had heard about their reputation as musicians, so they prodded the Jews as they worked: "Hey, sing us one of the songs of Zion!" The Jews winced. "How shall we sing the Lord's song in a strange land?" they answered (Psalm 137:4 KJV).

That's what you may be saying today. "How can I sing when I feel so blue?" But the Lord said, "Make a joyful noise unto the Lord." Even if you can't sing, you can at least hum or whistle—anything to get the music flowing. While the first notes may be teary or shaky, you'll get better as you go along.

Music soothes the troubled beast within us. It blows the dust off our spirits. Saul, entangled in his depression, was cheered by David's harp. That's why many doctors' offices have soft music playing. That's why companies use recorded music on telephone "holds." Music soothes irritated customers or anxious clients.

What kind of music is best for you? I cannot answer that. You may prefer the classics, some of which were written by great composers like Schumann, Mozart, or Tchaikovsky in times of their own depression. Others prefer more lively, toe-tapping music. Many choose gospel music. The important thing is that you *make* time to listen.

When I was growing up, my family listened to WHAS in Louisville. Every school morning at 6:30, WHAS played band music; I was awakened to rousing Sousa marches. What a way to start the day! That's one reason we have marching bands at football games and pep bands at basketball games.

A rich musical charge can electrify an audience and a team.

General George Rogers Clark, a great frontier general, had to have his leg amputated. In 1816 there were few surgical procedures to comfort the patient—just a crude hacking off of the leg.

Just as the surgeon began, up marched the regimental band, stopping outside the window. They played heartily as the surgeon cut off the general's leg. General Clark tapped his fingers on the tabletop to the beat of the music. Music makes a difference.

I need music; you need music. Music is one of God's common gifts to us. Buy good albums and cassettes, and get a good FM radio. Listen to the mellow stations. Put up your feet and relax. Let your soul resonate.

Music will not completely eliminate your depression, but it can make a big difference.

You may not be able to sing good, but you can always sing a good song!

What a Difference
a Vacation Makes!

We didn't take vacations when I was a child, but we did get a lot of those "having a wonderful time, wish you were here!" postcards. I bet you did too. People on vacation are expected to spend some time writing postcards to people they are trying to get away from.

But during my first year in high school, my dad bought a new car and announced that we were going on vacation. So we hopped in the car, fearing that this was only a dream. For three whole days we saw how many miles we could put on the car. But we beat the postcards home.

To my dad, vacations were a luxury. Vacations were times to work in his garden, paint the house, and do various projects he could not get to the rest of the year.

I'm different. Vacations are a necessity for me. If God rested, so should humans. We need to vacate the familiar.

Elijah needed a vacation—badly. Without blinking an eye he had killed hundreds of priests of Baal. But then one harangue by the wicked Jezebel sent the fatigued prophet running with his eyes back over his shoulder. He fell under a tree and moaned, "I have had enough, Lord."

Today a lot of Christians will say, "Lord, I have had enough!"

One reason my dad didn't take vacations was that he modeled his life after our pastors, who didn't believe in vacations. They often laughed, "The Devil doesn't take vacations, does he?"

But it was a long time before I learned the punch line: "and that's what makes him the Devil!"

Vacations are not luxuries. They are psychological necessities. A significant portion of spiritual depression in America could be eliminated by *good* vacations. Sometimes that means vacations for husband and wife without the children, without driving 500 miles, without spending an enormous amount of money on Visa and MasterCards. Sometimes it might not even be exotic.

Vacations stretch our minds and rejuvenate our spirits.

Vacations offer us new memories.

Vacations make our daily routines more bearable.

"We'll work till Jesus comes" is the theme song of many evangelical workaholics. Yet in reality many of them work until they drop. And sometimes they don't get up.

While Jesus probably did not take "vacations," He definitely did make and take time to get away from the pressure, from the demands, from the crowds. He did vacate.

Be good to yourself: Vacate. It will all be there when you get back. But the you that you bring home will be more capable of dealing with the things that complicate, cause, and prolong depression.

What a Difference
a Memory Makes!

Memories can either stimulate or eliminate depression. Every day offers you the opportunity to create the memories that will either warm you or chill you. An experience or incident becomes positive or negative *by your choice.*

- A widow may be depressed by memories of her husband, especially on red-letter days: an anniversary or a birthday.
- A ill person may be depressed by memories of healthier days.
- An underemployed or unemployed person may be depressed by memories of other jobs or news of promotions for friends.
- A mother with an empty nest may be depressed by memories of busy days with children underfoot.
- A husband in a troubled marriage may be depressed by memories of better days.

Memories are one of God's creative gifts. That's one reason why Americans are such camera buffs; pictures are ways of preserving the memory. The mind is overwhelmed by present problems, so the pictures act as a prod: "Remember when..."

But memories can also provoke depression. Sometimes it is a song, a smell, a name, or a place that starts the search through the brain's filing system. Suddenly the shadows roll in.

Some depressed people collect bad memories. They scowl,

"Don't think I'm going to forget this!" So they replay the insult, the injury, the spoiled occasion in slow motion, reliving every detail. Again, that's part of choosing.

Memories, according to David Seamands, are like paintings in an art gallery: They hang there, bathed in light, waiting to be seen. We walk through the gallery's darkness, pausing here, lingering there, shuddering sometimes, then moving on. But occasionally we stop and look back one more time.[73]

Jesus is anxious to walk with us through that gallery. He carefully studies our glances and glares. Sometimes He stops. "This one bothers you, doesn't it?" He asks.

We nod and look away.

He steps forward, firmly taking hold of the picture. Then He lifts. When we look up, the wall is bare.

Museums and art galleries have large collections stored for eventual exhibit; most rotate pictures. When one picture goes off exhibit, they select another to replace it in the gallery.

Deep in the subconscious mind we have stored pictures. Some are good, some are bad. But you choose what will be exhibited.

It does take time for some of the memories to diffuse and fade, but it is easier if we crowd out the bad memories with good ones. Don't think of your husband in the hospital suffering, I suggested to one widow. Rather, see him at his height, chopping wood on a cold November morning. Select a positive memory.

Decide to limit the bad memories: "You get one minute today—not one second longer." Now call up the good memory. Invite it to hang around awhile longer. Replay it one more time.

Remember this: *Today* is a good day to create tomorrow's memories.

What a Difference
a Nap Makes!

As previously noted, one of the symptoms of depression is insomnia or any sleep disturbance, such as delayed insomnia or frequent waking during the night. Sleep is one way to mask depression. It is possible to put the hours in bed and get up more exhausted than when you went to bed.

Have you ever lain in the darkness rehashing the problem until sleep seemed impossible? Some depressed people don't count sheep; they rehash grievances and misfortunes. They replay failure tapes.

Sleep has come under attack by some of the high-energy motivation speakers: "Why lie in bed? The day's a-wasting! There are deals to be made, sales to be rung up, profits to be banked!"

Indeed, one recent book asks, "Why sleep at all?" The author describes sleep as just another bad habit. Successful people have to squeeze every minute of productivity and possibility out of the working day. Naps are for children, the author scoffs, not go-getters!

But sleep is a God-given gift. The psalmist—who battled depression—noted, "He grants sleep to those he loves" (Psalm 127:2). Even secular scientists recognize the need for quality sleep as a time to replace dying cells. Some scientists believe that special substances are manufactured during sleep. Others report that the synapses (those "bridges" between brain cells) are cleaned during sleep.

However, television offers an alternative. Why sleep when you can watch one of the hundred channels on cable, or see a movie that you missed in 1956 or 1966? There's always

The Tonight Show, followed by Nightline, followed by the Late Movie...

If you can't sleep at 2 A.M. you can get up and watch the all-news channel. And some of those stories will keep you from going back to sleep!

Sleep patterns have been drastically challenged in our world, particularly through shift work. Some workers have become depressed because of our tampering with the biological time clocks deep within us.

For three years I had a colleague who insisted on an afternoon nap. "Naps are good for you," he insisted. Naps offer psychological time-outs that we need in the midst of a tension-packed day. We need to take a hint from our Southern neighbors, who take their siestas seriously.

"Oh, but in this dog-eat-dog world, I'm vulnerable if I take a nap. The business deal of a lifetime might pass me by!" Hardly.

Actually, it's more likely that you think better *after* a nap, so that what looks like a rather ordinary business deal becomes the deal of a lifetime.

I wonder how many accidents and feuds and arguments and assaults could have been avoided by a nap.

Dr. Laverne Johnson of the Naval Health Research Center in San Diego warns, "It's probably true that most of us can get by on thirty to sixty minutes less sleep than we usually get. But generally we have to pay that back at some point."[74] One penalty is depression.

In research sponsored by the American Cancer Society, Dan Kripke found that the more your sleep pattern departs from the norm of seven to eight hours, the more likely you are to die. Kripke studied a million Americans between 1960 and 1966 and discovered that those who slept six to seven hours a night have a mortality rate 13 percent higher than those who sleep eight hours a night!

Of those persons who slept only five to six hours, 20 percent more have died. Kripke's conclusion: the less sleep, the higher the death percentages.[75]

Remember your dad snoozing on the couch. He wasn't being lazy. If a band of marauding Indians had happened into your neighborhood, he could have swung into action in a split second. And remember how much more lovable your dad was *after* a nap—and what happened if he was interrupted?

Do yourself a favor (and your mate, your children, your friends, and your employees). Take a nap!

What a Difference a Hobby Makes!

Stamps? Coins? Butterflies? Quilts? Antiques? "Hobbies?" the questionnaires always ask. "Too busy," we mumble. Some contemporary advocates of the Puritan work ethic question the validity of hobbies: "Better not to waste time."

But many parents have breathed easier because of hobbies which evaporate boredom and restlessness. Some people's hobbies have even turned into investments and jobs. One man sold his high-pressure construction business to devote full time to his hobby: collecting (and now selling) autographs of celebrities. And a hobby made Grandma Moses into a household word.

Hobbies soothe. In the height of World War II, Winston Churchill painted. During his presidency, Dwight Eisenhower painted and played golf. In retirement, Jimmy Carter has become a highly skilled woodworker. Hobbies should be recognized, says psychologist Barbara Holland, "as opportunities to add something to the world that didn't exist before." It may be a poem, a blanket, a cake, or a shell ornament. "To be able to change things and make things is a marvelous lightener of spirits.[76]

Hobbies cause us to take ourselves less seriously. Sometimes hobbies are a bridge—later abandoned but appreciated. Hobbies, when taken seriously, lead us out of self-preoccupation and into the world of other people. We share what we have created or collected or learned. We exchange ideas and insights and techniques. We admire the skills of others.

Hobbies, for the depressed person, can be a way of

crafting "thank-you's." One cold Kansas City Sunday, my afternoon nap was interrupted by persistent knocking at my front door. I got up and discovered a counselee.

"Come in," I invited. He immediately complimented my Christmas tree. "Ah," I thought, "he's probably lonely because he's experiencing his first Christmas alone."

"I brought you something," he said, holding out a small box. I opened the package and found a small stained-glass ornament. "I made it myself," he said proudly.

In his depression he bought a stained-glass-making kit to make his Christmas gifts. But the hobby became a healing, creative time. As I write this, I turn in my chair and watch the sun stream through his ornament. I am reminded that he has survived his depression and his divorce. He has since remarried and graduated from seminary, and today he pastors a thriving congregation. Through his depression he became a stronger believer and a gentler servant of God.

His parishioners can afford to let him see their wounds; he understands.

Hobbies may cost something, but they are therapeutic. A hobby is money well invested.

What a Difference
a Counselor Makes!

One reason why depression is so common is the difficulty of finding a good counselor, one who will respond authentically and compassionately and who will listen not only to symptoms.

How can you find a good counselor? Ask your clergymen, your family doctor, or your Mental Health Association. Depending on the nature of your need, they may refer you to a psychiatrist, psychologist, social worker, or other counselor, either in private practice or in a community mental health center.

Maybe some of these titles seem confusing to you.

- *Psychiatrist*: A physician with four years of advanced training emphasizing human behavior who diagnoses and treats mental disorders.
- *Psychologist*: A nonphysician with graduate training in human behavior, usually possessing a doctoral degree such as Ph.D.
- *Psychiatric social worker*: An individual trained in providing social and human services. Many hold at least a master's degree.
- *Counselor*: A person trained in counseling and guidance who works in the mental-health field.
- *Psychoanalyst*: A person, usually a psychiatrist or psychologist, who treats patients by talking with them in an attempt to bring their unconscious conflicts and defenses to the surface.
- *Therapist*: A person trained in a variety of therapeutic

techniques for dealing with human behavior. Educational backgrounds are diverse.[77]

Counseling is a major avenue to healing. The counselor cannot heal you, but a skilled counselor may be the means that God has chosen to help you. A skilled Christian counselor is in partnership with God to bring healing to you. The Spirit-guided counselor admits that he has little to do with a person's actual healing; he is merely a vessel through whom God works.

Remember, God does not always work quickly, but He does work thoroughly.

Remember also that depression does not contradict your Christian testimony.

> The greatest of all God's saints have variously experienced instant healing, progressive healing, partial healing, and no healing. God will not be limited to our methods, timing, and desires. He remains unpredictable . . . if we could predict him he would cease to be God or we would be divine.[78]

God may choose to use a skilled secular counselor, since not all Christian counselors are prepared by disposition or training to deal with depression. We are fortunate to have a cadre of skilled counselors, but we must use caution in selecting any counselor, whether Christian or secular.

The Christian counselor must be trained, and he or she must do more than merely prescribe Scripture verses! One cannot estimate how many persons' depression has been deepened by well-intentioned but ill-trained counselors, those whose methods of
- *pray* more
- *praise* more
- *give* more
- *do* more

have only shackled the depressed.

GOAL 6 ❖ HELPING THE DEPRESSED

Hints for Helpers: Everyone Gets a Little Blue

Depression is almost as common as the common cold; in fact, it may be its mental equivalent. There is no reason for you or anyone else to keep depression "in the closet."

While everyone gets a *little* depressed, some people get more than a little depressed; they drift into *deep* depression. They may become paralyzed, incapable of functioning.

How many times have you visited a sick person and ended up swapping symptoms and comparing medications? It's depressing, in visitation, to have someone pull out his pills and start practicing medicine on the spot. When you're with a depressed person, consider his or her needs.

Some people became clinically depressed because no one recognized their depression, or else someone downplayed it. In their own strength they attempted to "pop psych" themselves out of difficulty. Some were simply too frightened to admit their depression.

I am not good at repairs, but I know a good repairman. His attitude is "Please admit your limitation. It is so much easier and cheaper when I don't have to correct another person's tinkering." Remember, you're a *helper*—not a psychologist, doctor, or druggist.

As a friend and helper, following these hints, *you* can make a difference!

Hints for Helpers: Withhold Commentary

- "You should..."
- "If I were you, I'd..."
- "Your problem is..."
- "Snap out of it!"
- "If you ask me..."

It's amazing what "helpers" say to the depressed. Your best gift may be silence. It's so tempting to declare martial law and set the depressed straight. In fact, some counselors' approach is straightforward, no holds barred. But the counselee limps away, more wounded than healed.

Chuck Colson observes, "We tend to think we have to go into lengthy, detailed, elaborate explanations with eighteen steps. Or we go to the other extreme, which is to reduce things to simple formulas."[79]

When the prodigal son returned, his father chose to withhold his commentary. Although the son had a rehearsed speech, the father ignored it.

The gift of silence can make a big difference.

Never speak unless you can improve on silence.

Hints for Helpers:
Be Hospitable

Sometimes angels have to be caterers. Remember Elijah getting room service in the midst of his depression? Remember Jesus being attended by angels after His temptation?

Paul depended upon the hospitality of other people. Time and again Paul commented on the graciousness of others:

- Greet Rufus... and his mother, who has been a mother to me, too (Romans 16:13).
- I commend to you our sister Phebe... for she has been a great help to many people, including me (Romans 16:1,2).
- Gaius, whose hospitality I and the whole church here enjoy (Romans 16:23).
- Your love has given me great joy and encouragement, because you, brother, have refreshed the hearts of the saints (Philemon 7).

The writer of Hebrews suggests that we not only entertain friends but that we also "not forget to entertain strangers, for by so doing some people have entertained angels without knowing it" (Hebrews 13:2). You do not have to know the depressed person to be kind and gracious to him.

Perhaps you could be someone's caterer today by sharing hospitality. Depressed people forget to eat. The widow doesn't want to eat alone because each bite reminds her of her loss. She avoids preparing his favorite dishes, and there are no longer any compliments for a good meal. But she needs to eat to have strength to fight the depression. A meal *at your table* would provide nourishment and a new memory. It could be just what the doctor ordered.

Hospitality is a seed planted, a dollar saved for a rainy day.

I remember how hard it was for me to come home in the afternoons to an empty townhouse. Many nights I worked late at the office—anything to avoid the absence of walking through the door and smelling something good cooking.

Some nights after I got home my neighbors would call: "Come on down. Made too much food tonight."

"It could be used as leftovers."

"No. Need to eat it up!"

Some nights it was a meal and other nights a dessert and iced tea, but it always included conversation. My neighbors didn't have degrees in psychology or certificates that hung on the wall; they simply had *and practiced* the gift of hospitality.

We've become so restaurant-orientated. Sometimes restaurants are too loud, too public, too crowded, too plastic to be the right place. Sometimes your dining room becomes a Bethel, the place where God comes.

You may have to insist and persist in offering hospitality. You may have to say an equivalent of "pretty please." And they may say no. But don't take any no to always mean no. Ask again and again.

It doesn't have to be fancy or elaborate. Soup and sandwich, pie and coffee, or ice cream and fresh fruit could be as effective as a tranquilizer or antidepressant.

Simple acts of hospitality may produce compound positive results. Sometimes we can *do* when we don't know what to say. "Silver and gold have I none," said Peter, "but such as I have give I you" (Acts 3:6 KJV).

Your act of hospitality, dramatic or common, could be just what the doctor ordered.

Hints for Helpers:
Be Practical

Many of us long for a dramatic ministry gift. But Scripture assures us that simple things, like a cup of cold water, are valued.

It's easy to wring our hands and say, "I wish I could do something to help" or "I don't know what to do." Many times we are ineffective in helping because we overlook the common, the ordinary.

Or we pray, "O God, help Betty. You know she's depressed." But perhaps God has chosen *you* to answer your own prayer. Perhaps *you* are to help Betty.

Fran, 48, does not have a green thumb. Her husband teases that she can kill a plant by looking at it. Yet she had been burdened by her friend, Alice, a recent widow. Alice and her husband had been incredible gardeners; in fact they had spent hours together digging, planting, pruning, and enjoying. But in the three weeks since Alice's husband died, Alice has not stepped foot outside her house.

Then one morning Fran knocked on her door. Alice laughed softly when she saw Fran's outfit. "Why are you dressed like that?"

"I've come to work in your garden." Alice protested, but Fran slipped by her and headed through the house toward the backdoor leading to the garden. Soon Alice joined her. They spent the morning hoeing, raking, pulling weeds, and picking beans but also singing, praying, and at times sobbing.

All day they worked and shared. That night Alice slept well for the first time since her husband's death. The next morning she looked at the strawberries and vegetables harvested the day before, and said, "I can't eat all of this!"

Then she thought of Fran. "I'll bake them a fresh strawberry pie." Slowly, as she worked in her kitchen, her mood lifted. Now the garden is her delight.

Bill was troubled by a depressed friend who wouldn't talk. So he invited him to play racquetball. His friend resisted but finally said yes. While the game didn't challenge Bill's skills, it did give him a chance to minister and to reach out to his friend.

If you're not good at the fantastic, use the common. But be practical.

John said that we ought to lay down our lives for our brothers. In John's day that was a real possibility. In our own day the least we can do is be inconvenienced. Many depressed people are reluctant to ask for help, so sometimes we have to ask on their behalf.

John believed this intensely, and it led him to ask how the love of God could be in someone who ignores another person's needs.

John removed the excuse of saying, "I'm too busy ministering." He said, "*If anyone*"—whether leader or follower—"has resources..." by all means let him help.

Let the Holy Spirit nudge you to share your resources. Let the Holy Spirit be creative through you.

May it not be said of you—

- I was *hungry* and you read cookbooks to me.
- I was *naked* and you showed me clothes catalogs.
- I was *cold* and you showed me slides of Hawaii.
- I was *alone* and you gave me tickets to a football game.
- I was *afraid* and you sang, "You'll Never Walk Alone!"

It takes practice to be practical, but it *does* make a difference.

Hints for Helpers:
Affirm

Self-talk taunts many depressed people. We laugh or joke about "the funny farm" or "the men in white coats" or "the nuthouse." All are degrading cliches. Some depressed people grew up in families that had psychologically troubled persons who were ignored. Some families disguised their problems. Yet a child concluded, "That's how they would treat *me* if I had a mental problem."

So we pretend. We resist. We deny. As a result, some psychological problems get worse. If there had been early intervention, the pain and consequences could have been minimal.

Few of us receive as much affirmation as we need for normal growth. Some of us grew up in families slow to praise, quick to condemn—either by statement or by silence. Some of us grew up in homes where criticism was brutal and swift.

As a result, we mimic that self-talk and continuously replay the accusing cassettes.

For those who come from "put-down" Christian homes, the statement "If you were really a Christian you wouldn't be depressed!" rips through the linings of their hearts.

In their minds they do not have good alternatives.

If I tell you about my depression, you might criticize, condemn, or unchristianize me. So I will have to endure the pain in silence.

> If I don't tell you about my depression, the burden will only get heavier.

There is a point, a threshold, at which the pain becomes too great to be carried.

So the depressed person wonders, "What does my depression say about my faith?"

Nothing.

To the depressed we need to say:

- I love you.
- I affirm you.
- I don't judge you.
- I believe in you.

Some depressed individuals will have to hear your affirmation several times before they begin to believe it. They have been put down so often that they will question your motives.

But unconditional love, given freely, could resolve a great deal of depression in our world. Not—

- I love you *because*. . .
- I love you *if*. . .
- I'll love you *when*. . .

but I love you, *period.* That phrase is so rare, even in Christian families. And what we learn from our families translates into our theology of God.

Some have concluded:

> God loves me when I am perfect or
> when I am no longer depressed.

Rather, the Word teaches that *while we were sinners* God loved us and gave His Son for us. There is no "trial period" or probation to see how we handle God's grace.

The agenda for the church and for believers is to affirm and love depressed people, to dispense big dosages of acceptance and caring. Part of affirmation is applauding the first baby steps, the first signs of progress.

Hints for Helpers:
Read

Paul wrote Timothy "to bring me my parchments" or books. We're fortunate today to have such a knowledge of depression. For so many years the depressed were subjected to ignorance and mistreatment and bias. You have the opportunity at the nearest library to read up on depression. Both theoretical and practical information is readily available.

To do your best means working at gaining insight into depression. It means rejecting folklore and old wives' tales. It may mean wading through some heavy psychologese. But an idea, a phrase, may be a kernel that will grow into a healthy plant. You may have access to resources that no one else has. Maybe it wasn't coincidence that you read a particular article or book. One article could change your attitude!

As prevalent as depression is, you need to read up on the subject. Eight to ten persons out of every 100, or 25 million Americans, will experience severe depression during their lifetime. Some of those are your neighbors or colleagues or friends. God will bring depressed people into your life so that you can plant a seed of encouragement. You want to be more than a dispenser of platitudes, don't you? You want to help!

An article helped one friend. I found it in an old magazine, and as I read it I thought of him. I clipped it and dropped it in the mail. "It was as if that author had me in mind," he wrote back.

Many times I've dropped a copy and a note into the mail.

But *first* I know the content of the article. Sometimes I've highlighted or marked a particular passage, knowing that some people are too depressed to read the whole article. Sometimes the highlighted passage whets their appetite.

Remember, it is often a single paragraph, sentence, or phrase (rather than the entire article) that makes the difference.

Hints for Helpers:
Confess

"What would you know about depression?" Has anyone ever said that to you in a bitter, sarcastic tone?

You could respond, "I'll never understand if you don't talk to me about *your* depression." That type of response leads to acceptance. That's why your doctor asks about your symptoms. He hasn't had every disease he treats, but as you explain your symptoms, he recognizes a pattern and makes a diagnosis.

You could repond, "Let me share my experience with you." But there are risks with this kind of approach. One patient asked a minister, "Have you ever been depressed?"

"Yes."

"Then tell me about it," she ordered.

"When I was seven, my dog died and I was depressed."

The patient shrieked and stalked out of the office. "I'm depressed because my husband left me, and he says he understands because his dog died!"

Too many Christians are closet depressives. We've been afraid to admit our depression. We assume that it contradicts our testimony or witness, that we are depressed because we aren't trusting Jesus enough or because there is some spiritual gift that we haven't sought or received. That's what we fear someone will say if we are transparent about our depression.

But confession is good for the soul, and it may be just the encouragment someone needs. More people would be healed of depression if more people admitted it, particularly Christian celebrities. I also think more of us would be healed if we knew people whom God has chosen to heal over the long haul rather than instantaneously.

Everyone is a moon and has a dark side that he or she never shows to anyone, says Sharon Matthews, a California counselor. We edit our life stories to gain acceptance but also to avoid rejection. But by so doing, we eliminate our potential to be used of the Lord to bring healing.

As a helper you may feel led to share out of your own past. That may be a bit unnerving or unpleasant.

Your yesterday is someone's today!

God doesn't heal us to silence our prayers. He heals us so that we may share with other people the comfort we have received ourselves (2 Corinthians 1:4).

Your confession might be the word of hope that a depressed person needs to hear today.

Hints for Helpers: Reject
Simple Answers & Solutions

So many books on a Christian understanding of mental health offer 1, 2, 3's. They are like the doctor who says, "Take two aspirin and get some rest. You'll feel better in the morning."

Some people laboriously follow the steps, but the problem worsens rather than improves. So they try harder.

Have you ever failed to lose weight on a certain diet? "Can't fail—you'll lose it." So you copied down the notes and couldn't wait for the new you: 10 to 20 pounds lighter. But those battles with the scales continued. Didn't you feel deprived and depressed when that system failed?

Here are some ways to reject the simple answers.

1. Don't pat depressed people on the head and say, "There, there! You'll be all right."

2. Watch your tone of voice and body expressions. Impatience is easy to spot.

3. Edit your happiness. Save your glowing reports of all the good, wonderful, incredible things that are going on in your life. They will only further depress the wounded. Remember Job wishing that his comforters would go away and leave him alone?

4. Think about how your words translate into the experience of the depressed. Solomon as a teacher searched for just the right words (Ecclesiastes 12:10). Many times we are so anxious to say something that we wind up saying nothing.

Right words heal. Wrong words wound.

If you've read up on the subject of depression, if you share your concern, you're more likely to say the right thing.

> **Simple answers are the products of simple minds!**

Hints for Helpers: Be Patient

"When am I going to get over this?" That's a common question asked by depressed individuals.

Hopefully, through this book, the depression will be reduced in intensity, frequency, and duration. God chooses to heal on His own timetable. Why didn't He remove Paul's thorn? Were Paul's prayers ineffective? Paul has been with the Lord about 1900 or so years. I doubt that he thinks much about this thorn these days!

God is transforming our lowly, depressed minds and bodies. The problem is patience.

As a child, did you ever put inch marks on the wall? You stood with your back against the wall, and your parents marked the spot and dated it. But now it's hard for you to imagine ever having been so short. Yet you were—the mark and the date say so!

As with our physical growth, so it is with emotional and spiritual growth. You're growing. You're not the same person you were when you began reading this book. As the mind stretches to accommodate new thoughts, it never goes back to its original limitations.

We're often depressed because we want to avoid the terrible, the awful, the unpleasant.

A helper must recognize the impatience of a depressed person. A helper must applaud his or her baby steps toward patience.

In a world that wants instant tea and coffee, instant pudding, and instant replay, many people ask, ''How do you spell relief?''

''T-I-M-E!''

Hints for Helpers:
Reach Out

Why does God comfort us?

   ____   To answer our prayers?
   ____   To solve our problems?
   ____   Because He loves us?
   ____   So that we can help others?
   ____   All of the above?
   ____   None of the above?

It's natural for a Christian to praise the Lord. He has touched us and healed us. Paul begins his second letter to the Corinthians, "Praise be to the God and Father of our Lord Jesus Christ, who comforts us in all our troubles." (1:3,4). We have a tendency to stop there. What a great verse!

Paul, however, chose a comma rather than a period.

"God comforts us," Paul noted, "*so that* we can comfort those in *any* trouble with the comfort we ourselves have received from God" (1:4). But as long as depression remains in the closet, with those who have been comforted going undercover, it's hard to share the comfort. The depressed become more depressed because God's plan is not being implemented.

Ask yourself, "What do I want to learn from my depression?" When Jacob wrestled with the angel, he groaned, "I will not let you go until you bless me!" Are you willing to wrestle with depression until it blesses you, so that you can help others? Or will you opt for the shortcut?

To those would-be helpers who protest, "I'm not a psychologist!" here are some helpful hints.[80]

- *Stay in Touch.* Be there. As a friend you're now more important than ever.
- *Touch.* A hug or a simple squeeze of the hand lets a person know that you care.
- *Call Before You Visit.* The depressed individual may not feel up to a visitor. Don't be afraid to call another time.
- *Weep* with the depressed if they weep. Laugh when they laugh. Don't interrupt the silence.
- *Go* for a walk or an outing.
- *Include* the depressed in your holiday plans.
- *Remember* the other family members. They may need a break or a bit of encouragement. A mate of a depressed person may desperately need to talk.
- *Be Creative.* Share books, periodicals, taped music, posters, or home-baked goods.
- *Ask.* Don't be reluctant to ask about depression. But the depressed person may be reluctant to talk, so give him an out: "Do you feel like talking about it?"
- *Volunteer to Chauffeur.* The depressed person may need a ride to a counselor or for shopping. The depressed person may avoid something because he or she doesn't want to drive or doesn't wish to go alone.
- *Compliment.* Depressed people sometimes ignore grooming. Don't lie, but look for something to compliment.
- *Accept* their anger. Depressed people may become angry for no obvious reason. Don't take everything they say personally.
- *Help* with household chores. Take out the laundry, wash the dishes, water the plants. You don't have to do it all, but you can help. But first ask.
- *Send Cards* that say "I do care." Make it personal by including a P.S.
- *Don't Lecture* the depressed person if he seems to

213

be using his depression for personal advantage.

- *Talk About the Future.* Hope is important. Encourage the depressed person to dream.
- *Keep Positive.* It's contagious.
- *Share News.* Discuss the news. Clip articles that you think might interest the depressed person. Don't let him think the world is passing him by.
- *Don't Expect Gratitude.*
- *Pray* for the depressed and also pray *with* the depressed.
- *Go* the second mile.
- *Applaud* the first step.

Hints for Helpers:
Pray

Paul Tournier, a Swiss psychiatrist, observed that the sad thing about many "I'll pray for you's" is that they often remain nothing more than a well-meant expression of concern—a spiritual cliche.

How many times have you prayed, "Lord, help Mrs. Jones. You know the struggle she's going through"?

How many times has the Lord whispered, "Why don't you help Mrs. Jones?" Americans have the capacity to answer most of their own prayers—at least those that deal with financial concerns. Yet we keep asking God to do it. We are called to be conduits through which God works to answer prayer.

We need to "underwrite" our prayers—to ask God to make us more aware of the resources in our lives that He would be pleased to use.

I have a prayer book with 31 pages. Listed on each page are specific names and needs that I need to pray about. I think of one depressed person on a salt-free diet. Sometimes, when I reach for the saltshaker, I retract my hand as a way of "bearing his burden."

Recently, with a depressed person, I opened my prayer book and showed him his name. I wanted him to know that his name was there as a way of encouraging him. "But, " I added, "I don't wait until the seventeenth day to pray for you, but also as you come to mind."

We're busy people with good intentions but overloaded minds and packed agendas.

Depressed people need to know that the words "I'll pray

for you" are more than a spiritual pat on the head. Sometimes when I don't know what to say or think or do, it helps to know that my Father does know. If I have listened to a depressed person, I may know particular times or circumstances that trigger his depression. So I can pray anticipating that depression.

Praying for people is a big commitment, but a necessary one. Your prayer commitment can make a difference.

Hints for Helpers:
Celebrate

The prodigal's father was obviously distressed about his son's choices. In fact, if he was much of a father at all, he must have been depressed.

One way he dealt with his depression was by anticipating reconciliation. He selected a calf and began fattening it. As he fed the calf, he no doubt patted it and said, "Someday you'll be the banquet feast—when my boy comes home!"

Eventually the son came home. The verse says that "While he was still a long way off" the father swung into action— he ran to his son! At the first sign of return, the father rejoiced. There was no probation period, no 30-day observation period to see if he had really changed. The father didn't wait with folded arms saying "We'll see!"

As a helper, you need to celebrate the victory even though the depressed person is still a long way off. In fact, your celebration might stimulate more progress.

"What's to celebrate?" you ask.

- Celebrate small successes.
- Celebrate often.
- Celebrate yourself when you've chosen not to be depressed.
- Celebrate when a situation that would once have provoked major depression sparks only a temporary depression.

You must not wait for six depressionless months before you celebrate. Six days might qualify!

Hints for Helpers: Holiday Depression

Holidays are family times. Yet for many people holidays can be depressing because someone with whom they have created Christmas memories is absent, whether through death, divorce, or separation. For many people there is one less present to buy, hide, and wrap. But this also means one less present to receive, one less surprise, one less memory.

Peter "celebrated" his first Christmas alone last year. His family had gone out of their way not to mention Beth's absence. "Someone say something!" seemed on every family member's tongue as they gathered for the traditional family Christmas Eve. They figuratively tiptoed around Peter, fearing that someone might accidentally mention Beth's name.

Finally a niece, too young to understand, simply asked, "Where's Aunt Beth?" The question ricocheted through everyone's heart. Grandmother swiftly whisked her away for a cookie.

During this family time suicide rates and hospitalizations increase. Some people cannot pretend that their disappointments and hurts are not there.

Here are some suggestions for helping.

1. If you adopt a "whatever you do, don't mention his name" rule, you'll make conversation strained and unnatural.
2. Consider some new times or locations for activities. Maybe this is the year to celebrate on Christmas Eve rather than on the morning of the twenty-fifth. Perhaps

a meal in a restaurant or another family member's home would be wise.

3. If you keep old traditions, give the grieving ones an opportunity to say no or to limit their involvement. Don't wait until the day before the holiday to ask their plans. Make sure you tell them that you still want them to participate. The wounded, in fact, may feel alienated while everyone else is having "such a good time." Some will feel guilty that they are hampering everybody's festivity.

4. Don't insist that old traditions be completed. Traditions which produce a flood of discomfort or stress are counterproductive. Give a grieving or depressed person a way (even at the last moment) to take a time-out or to say, "I'll think I'll pass."

Be cautious about dismissing a grieving person's feelings. Don't manipulate someone into celebrating: "If you're not here, it just won't be the same without you" or "I won't hear of you spending Christmas alone." Some people can feel alone even in the midst of a party.

Make holiday depression an opportunity to learn. Give the season a chance. Reach out and help someone.

Hints for Helpers: Widowhood

There are 12.5 million widows and widowers in this country—what I call "the ignored people." Oh, we take the casseroles to their homes, send them cards, order the beautiful flowers and make appearances at the funeral homes, but then we promptly forget about them.

Our "call me if you need anything" promises during the funeral period sound appropriate, but the time when widow/ers most need our help is often three weeks, three months, or three years after the flowers have gone.

But we expect them to return the casserole dishes, send out the thank-you notes, and get on with life. But some can't. The depression is too paralyzing.

In colonial days a widow had perhaps 30 days to grieve. Then she remarried someone, often selected by the elders of the church. In North Carolina, on occasion, the funeral for the first husband took place in the morning and the wedding to the second in the afternoon. Physical survival demanded the widow/ers "get hold of themselves." It was not uncommon for many colonists to have had three or four mates by age 35.

Depression is caused when "significant others" disappear from our lives after the death of a mate or child or friend. The living must walk through the valley of depression, which can be as frightening as the valley of the shadow of death.

Take a concordance and look up all the references to widows in the Bible. You'll be amazed by the number. Then look at the words of caution directed to those who neglect widows. James said that the essence of religion is not to build magnificent church buildings but to look after widows and orphans in their depression (James 1:27).

Widow/ers would be less depressed if we were there—if we sat in quiet living rooms or at hushed dining room tables listening to the sounds of grief. Widow/ers would be less depressed if we *still* included them in our foursomes for lunch or brunch. Widow/ers would be less depressed if we helped them dispose of clothing and personal items.

Widow/ers would be less depressed if we allowed them to wait instead of politely sniffle when they come back to busy schedules 30 days later to sit and listen to them. Ezekiel joined the exiles *where they were living* and "sat among them for seven days—overwhelmed" (Ezekiel 3:15).

Widows/ers would be less depressed if we allowed them to wait instead of politely sniffle when they come back to church. We never vocally insist, "Please hurry up and get over Ed's death," but we imply it with our silence and our glances. Too often our silence, because we don't know what to say, pushes the grieving further down the road to depression than anyone should ever have to go.

Our friendship with the grieving should be like those rest stops along the interstate highways—a place to pull over and rest before we resume the journey.

In His Time

Well, we've come to the end of our journey together. A few pages ago we were strangers; now we're friends. It's time to take the Depression Inventory again. You'll be surprised by your progress!

This book has not pushed for overnight change. Depression doesn't just go "poof" and disappear. It is a tenant that defies eviction orders and fights for every inch of its territory. But in time it will yield.

Urban T. Holmes relates a powerful story about depression.

> A certain seminary professor's son died tragically, [and] he left the campus for a period. Upon his return, he appeared unexpectedly at a seminary dinner and spoke to those gathered. "Ladies and gentlemen," he said, "in the last few weeks I have been to the bottom. But I am happy to report that the bottom is solid."[81]

God will lift you from the bottom in His time!

DEPRESSION INVENTORY II

Carefully read through the following statements. Pick out the statement in the group that best describes the way you feel today, right now!

Read all the statements before you make a choice.

1. *SADNESS*

____ I do not feel sad
____ I feel blue or sad
____ I am blue or sad all the time
____ I am so sad or unhappy that it is quite painful
____ I am so sad or unhappy that I can't stand it

2. *PESSIMISM*

____ I am not particularly pessimistic or discouraged about the future
____ I feel discouraged about the future
____ I feel that I have nothing to look forward to
____ I feel that I won't ever get over my troubles
____ I feel that the future is hopeless and that things cannot improve

3. *SENSE OF FAILURE*

____ I do not feel like a failure
____ I feel I have failed more than the average person
____ I feel I have accomplished very little that is worthwhile
____ As I look back on my life all I see is failure
____ I feel I am a complete failure as a person

4. DISSATISFACTION

____ I am not particularly dissatisfied
____ I feel bored most of the time
____ I don't enjoy things the way I used to
____ I don't get satisfaction out of anything anymore
____ I am dissatisfied with everything

5. GUILT

____ I don't feel particularly guilty
____ I feel bad or unworthy a good part of the time
____ I feel quite guilty
____ I feel bad or unworthy practically all
    the time now
____ I feel as though I am very bad or worthless

6. EXPECTATION OF PUNISHMENT

____ I don't feel I am being punished
____ I have a feeling that something bad may happen
    to me
____ I feel I am being punished or will be punished
____ I feel I deserve to be punished
____ I want to be punished

7. SELF-DISLIKE

____ I don't feel disappointed in myself
____ I am disappointed in myself
____ I don't dislike myself
____ I am disgusted with myself
____ I hate myself

8. SELF-ACCUSATIONS

____ I don't feel I am any worse than anybody else
____ I am critical of myself for my weaknesses
    and mistakes
____ I blame myself for my faults
____ I blame myself for everything bad that happens

9. **SUICIDAL IDEAS**

____ I don't have any thoughts of harming myself
____ I have thoughts of harming myself but I wouldn't
follow through
____ I feel I would be better off dead
____ I feel my family would be better of if I
were dead
____ I have definite plans about committing suicide
____ I would kill myself if I could

10. **CRYING**

____ I don't cry any more than usual
____ I cry more now that I used to
____ I cry all the time now—I can't stop
____ I used to be able to cry but now I can't

11. **IRRITABILITY**

____ I am no more irritated now than I ever am
____ I get annoyed or irritated more easily than
I used to
____ I feel irritated all the time
____ I don't get irritated at all at things that used to
irritate me

12. **SOCIAL WITHDRAWAL**

____ I have not lost interest in other people
____ I am less interested in other people than I used
to be
____ I have lost most of my interest in other people
and have little feeling for them
____ I have lost all my interest in other people

225

13. *BODY-IMAGE CHANGE*

____ I don't feel I look any worse than I used to
____ I am worried that I am looking old or unattractive
____ I feel that there are permanent changes in my appetite and they make me unattractive
____ I feel that I am ugly or repulsive-looking

14. *WORK RETARDATION*

____ I can work about as well as before
____ It takes extra effort to get started at doing something
____ I don't work as well as I used to
____ I have to push myself very hard to do anything
____ I can't do my work at all

15. *INSOMNIA*

____ I can sleep as well as usual
____ I wake up more tired in the morning than I used to
____ I wake up 1-2 hours earlier than usual and find it hard to get back to sleep
____ I wake up early every day and can't get more than 5 hours of sleep

16. *FATIGUE*

____ I don't get any more tired than usual
____ I get tired more easily than I used to
____ I get tired from doing anything
____ I get too tired to do anything

17. *ANOREXIA*

____ My appetite is no worse than usual
____ My appetite is not as good as it used to be
____ My appetite is much worse now
____ I have no appetite at all anymore

18. **WEIGHT LOSS**

____ I haven't lost much weight, if any, lately
____ I have lost more than 5 pounds
____ I have lost more than 10 pounds
____ I have lost more than 20 pounds

19. **HEALTH**

____ I am no more concerned about my health than
usual
____ I am concerned about aches and pains or upset
stomach or constipation
____ I am so concerned with how I feel or what I feel
that it's hard to think of much else
____ I am completely absorbed in what I feel

20. **INDECISIVENESS**

____ I make decisions about as well as ever
____ I try to put off making decisions
____ I have great difficulty making decisions
____ I can't make any decisions anymore

21. **SEX DRIVE**

____ I have not noticed any recent change in interest
in sex
____ I am less interested in sex than I used to be
____ I am much less interested in sex now
____ I have lost interest in sex completely

Now go back to the front of the book and compare your first
depression test with this current one. Look for the areas in
which you have improved.

NOTES

1. Don Baker and Emery Nester, *Depression: Finding Hope and Meaning in Life's Darkest Shadow* (Portland: Multnomah, 1983), p. 43.

2. Patricia Teuting, Stephen H. Koslow, and Robert M.A. Hirschfield, *Science Reports: Special Report on Depression Research* (Rockland, MD: National Institute of Mental Health, 1981), p. 1.

3. Lesley Hazleton, *The Right to Feel Bad: Coming to Terms with Normal Depression* (Garden City: Doubleday, 1984), p. 80.

4. Aaron T. Beck, *Depression: Causes and Treatment* (Philadelphia: University of Pennsylvania, 1967), p. 5.

5. Stephen B. Oates, *Abraham Lincoln: The Man Behind the Myths* (New York: Harper and Row, 1984), p. 42.

6. Stephen F. Blumberg and Jack E. Hokanson, "The Effects of Another Person's Response Style on Interpersonal Behavior in Depression," in *Journal of Abnormal Psychology*, 92 (May 1983), pp. 196-209.

7. Raj K. Chopra, *Making A Bad Situation Good* (Nashville: Thomas Nelson, 1984), p. 142.

8. Elizabeth R. Skoglund, *To Anger, With Love* (San Francisco: Harper and Row, 1977), p. 89.

9. G.A. Young, "God Leads His Dear Children Along," in *Worship and Song* (Kansas City: N.P.H., 1980), p. 480.

10. Harold L. Bussell, *Unholy Devotion: Why Cults Lure Christians* (Grand Rapids: Zondervan, 1983).

11. Ross Phares, *Bible in Pocket, Gun in Hand* (Lincoln: University of Nebraska, 1963), p. 131.

12. Baker and Nester, *Depression*, p. 43.

13. David Brandt, *Is That All There Is?* (New York: Poseidon, 1984), p. 240.

14. Baker and Nester, *Depression*, p. 130.

15. Archibald Hart, *Depression: Coping and Caring* (Arcadia: Cope, 1981), p. 8.

16. Ibid., p. 82.

17. Ibid., p. 28.

18. Ibid., p. 29.

19. Ibid., p. 6.

20. American Psychiatric Association, *Diagnostic and Statistical Manual of Mental Disorders*, 3rd Ed. (Washington, D.C.: American Psychiatric Association, 1980), pp. 222-23.

21. James C. Coleman, James N. Butcher, and Robert C. Carson, *Abnormal Psychology and Modern Life*, 6th Ed. (Glenville: Scott Foresman, 1980), p. 370.

22. Beck, *Depression*, p. 5.

23. Mike Yaconelli, "Thou Shalt Have No Other Celebrities Before Thee," in *The Wittenburg Door* (Dec.-Jan. 1983-84), p. 31.

24. Jerome Kagan, *The Nature of a Child* (New York: Basic Books, 1984), p. 280.

25. "How to Deal with Mental Problems" (Arlington, VA: National Mental Health Association, 1980), p. 5.

26. Ibid., pp. 6-7.

27. "New Hope for the Depressed," in *U.S. News and World Report*, 94 (Jan. 24, 1983), p. 40.

28. Baker and Nester, *Depression*, p. 56.

29. Kagan, *Nature*, p. 280.

30. Urban T. Holmes, III, *Spirituality for Ministry* (San Francisco: Harper and Row, 1983), p. 158.

31. *Letters from Lillian* (Springfield, MO: Assemblies of God, Division of Foreign Missions, 1983), p. 42.

32. Ibid.

33. Paul Tournier, *The Whole Person in a Broken World* (New York: Harper and Row, 1964), p. 79.

34. Bertram S. Brown, "What You Should Know About Mental Depression," in *U.S. News and World Report*, 77 (Sept. 9, 1974), p. 40.

35. *Letters from Lillian*.

36. William Backus and Maria Chapian, *Telling Yourself the Truth* (Minneapolis: Bethany House, 1980), p. 45.

37. Karl Marx and Frederick Engels, *The Civil War in the United States* (New York: International, 1937), p. 60.

38. Katherine M. Jones, *Heroines of Dixie: Women Tell Their Stories of the War* (Westport, CT: Greenwood Press, 1955), p. 357.

39. Peter F. Drucker, *The Effective Executive* (New York: Harper and Row, 1966), p. 111.

40. Carl Malmquist, "Major Depression in Childhood: Why We Don't Know More," in *American Journal of Orthopsychiatry*, 53 (Apr. 1983), p. 262.

41. Ibid.

42. Marilyn Sargeant and Joye Swearingen, "Depressive Disorders: Causes and Treatment" (National Institute of Mental Health, 1981).

43. Ibid.

44. Jeffrey F. Cohn and Edward Z. Tronick, "Three-Month-Old Infants' Reaction to Simulated Maternal Depression," in *Child Development*, 54 (Feb. 1983), p. 192.

45. "Troubled Children: The Quest for Help," in *Newsweek*, 83 (Apr. 8, 1974), p. 58.

46. "When A Teenager Gets Really Depressed," in *Changing Times*, 36 (June 1982), pp. 27-28.

47. Edward W. McCranie and Judith Bass, "Childhood Family Antecedents of Despondency and Self-Criticism: Implications for Depression," in *Journal of Abnormal Psychology*, 93 (Feb. 1984), p. 4.

48. Coleman, *Abnormal Psychology*, p. 368.

49. Paul Hauck, *Overcoming Depression* (Philadelphia: Westminster, 1973), p. 24.

50. Blumberg and Hokanson, "Effects."

51. Beck, *Depression*, p. 36.

52. Irwin Ross, "Feelings of Inferiority," in *Sky* (May 1980), pp. 71-72.

53. Nathan S. Kline, *From Sad to Glad: Kline on Depression* (New York: Putnam, 1974), p. 36.

54. Baker and Nester, *Depression*, p. 57.

55. Allen Hadidian, *A Single Thought* (Chicago: Moody, 1981).

56. D. Martyn Lloyd-Jones, *Spiritual Depression: Its Causes and Care* (Grand Rapids: Eerdmans, 1972), p. 17.

57. Ibid.

58. Jonathan Edwards, ed., *The Life and Diary of David Brainerd* (Chicago: Moody, 1949), p. 105.

59. Ibid., p. 120.

60. Winifred Scheffler, "Mental Health Care: Editorial Research Reports," in *Congressional Quarterly*, 2 (Sept. 21, 1979), p. 691.

61. Ibid., p. 700.

62. Kline, *Sad to Glad*, p. 22.

63. Scheffler, "Mental Health Care," p. 680.

64. "New Hope for the Depressed," p. 42.

65. Ibid., p. 40.

66. Backus and Chapian, *Telling Yourself*, p. 93.

67. Phillips Brooks, *Christ the Light and Life* (New York: E.P. Dutton, 1905), p. 134.

68. Barbara Holland, "Depression Is the Pits—But You Don't Need Pills to Climb Out," in *McCalls*, 110 (Mar. 1983), p. 32.

69. Julia M. Klein, "Running Away from Depression," in *Ms.*, 11 (May 1983), p. 85.

70. Ibid.

71. David B. Herzog, Dennis K. Norman, Christopher Gordon, and Maura Pepose, "Sexual Conflict and Eating Disorders in 27 Males," in *American Journal of Psychiatry*, 141 (Aug. 1984), p. 989.

72. "I Had a Love Affair with Food—And It Nearly Killed Me," *Los Angeles Times* (July 8, 1984), Section 4, p. 14.

73. David Seamands, *Healing Damaged Emotions* (Wheaton: Victor Books, 1982).

74. Robert Ebisch, "Sleeping Sickness?" in *Ambassdor* (July 1984), p. 19.

75. Ibid.

76. Holland, "Depression," p. 32.

77. Scheffler, "Mental Health Care," p. 691.

78. Skoglund, *To Anger, With Love*, p. 85.

79. Kathy Doran David, "Charles W. Colson: Confronting Casual Christianity," in *Christian Writer*, 3 (July 1984), p. 12.

80. "When A Friend Has Aids" (New York: Chelsea Psychotherapy Associates, 1984).

81. Holmes, *Spirituality*, p. 134.

BIBLIOGRAPHY

BOOKS

Alexander, Franz G., and Sheldon T. Selesnick. *The History of Psychiatry: An Evaluation of Psychiatric Thought and Practice from Prehistoric Times to the Present.* New York: Harper and Row, 1966.

Chopra, Raj J. *Making A Bad Situation Worse.* Nashville: Thomas Nelson, 1984.

Curtis, George Tichnor. *Life of James Buchanan,* Vol. 1. New York: Harper and Row, 1883.

Drakeford, John. *Integrity Therapy.* Nashville: Broadman, 1967.

Green, Bernard. *Goodbye Blues: Breaking the Tranquilizer Habit the Natural Way.* New York: McGraw-Hill, 1981.

Hart, Archibald. *Depression: Coping and Caring.* Arcadia: Cope, 1981.

Marty, Martin. *Pilgrims in Their Own Land: 500 Years of Religion in America.* Boston: Little, Brown and Co., 1984.

Maxwell, Margaret. *A Passion for Freedom: The Life of Sharlot Hall.* Tucson: University of Arizona, 1982.

Messerli, Jonathan. *Horace Mann: A Biography.* New York: Knopf, 1972.

Minirth, Frank B., Paul D. Meier, and States V. Skipper. *100 Ways to Defeat Depression.* Grand Rapids: Baker, 1979.

Peachey, Laban. *Learning to Understand People.* Scottsdale, Pennsylvania: Herald Press, 1965.

Wood, Jane, and Sharon Matthews. *The Mood Menders Treasury.* Sacramento: self-published, 1984.

Wright, H. Norman. *Now I Know Why I'm Depressed.* Eugene: Harvest House, 1984.

JOURNAL ARTICLES

Alley, Lauren B., and Lynn Y. Abramson. "Learned Helplessness Depression and Illustration of Control." *Journal of Personality and Social Psychology* (June 1982), 42:1114-26.

Atkinson, A. Kathleen, and Annette U. Richel. "Postpartum Depression in Primiparous Parents." *Journal of Abnormal Psychology* (Feb. 1984), 93:115-19.

Brumback, Roger A., and R. Dennis Staton. "Learning Disability and Childhood Depression." *American Journal of Orthopsychiatry* (Apr. 1983), 53:269-81.

Dauber, Richard B. "Subliminal Psychodynamic Activation in Depression: or the Role of Autonomy Issues in Depressed College Women." *Journal of Abnormal Psychology* (Feb. 1984), 93:9-18.

Eaves, Greg, and A. John Rush. "Cognitive Patterns in Symptomatic and Remitted Unipolar Major Depression." *Journal of Abnormal Psychology* (Feb. 1984), 93:31-40.

Feather, N.T., and J.G. Barber. "Depressive Reactions and Unemployment." *Journal of Abnormal Psychology* (May 1983), 92:185-95.

Gotlib, Ian H. "Depression and General Psychopathology in University Students." *Journal of Abnormal Psychology* (Feb. 1984), 93:19-30.

Keith, Pat M., and Robert S. Schafer. "Employment Characteristics of Both Spouses and Depression in Two-Job Families." *Journal of Marriage and the Family* (Nov. 1983), 45:977-84.

Kramlinger, Keith G., David W. Swanson, and Toshihito Maruta. "Are Patients with Chronic Pain Depressed?" *American Journal of Psychology* (June 1983), 140:747-49.

Lin, Nan, and Alfred Dean. "Social Support and Depression." *Social Psychiatry* (1984), 19:83-91.

Pecheur, David Rochard, and Keith J. Edwards. "A Comparison of Secular and Religious Versions of Cognitive Therapy with

Depressed Christian College Students." *Journal of Psychology and Theology* (Spring 1984), 12:45-54.

Ross, Catherine E., John Mirowsky, and Joan Huber. "Dividing Work/Sharing Work and in Between: Marriage Patterns and Depression." *American Sociological Review* (Dec. 1983), 48:809-23.

Sweet, William. "Mental Health Care Reappraisal." *Congressional Quarterly*, Vol. 2, No. 7.

Veleber, David M., and Donald I. Templer. "Effects of Caffeine on Anxiety and Depression." *Journal of Abnormal Psychology* (Feb. 1984), 93:120-22.

Zuk, Gerald H. "Towards A Value Duffusion Theory of Depression." *International Journal of Family Therapy* (Fall 1983), 5:155-67.

MAGAZINES

Bauer, Michael. "Tight Money, Hard Times and Tension." *Kansas City Star* (Apr. 27, 1980).

"Coping with Dreams." *Science News* (Feb. 19, 1983), 123:126.

"Emotional Problems: Could Counseling Help You Cope?" *Better Homes and Gardens* (May 1984), 180.

"If You Have A Problem with Christmas." *U.S. News* (Dec. 19, 1983), 95:68.

Knox, Gerald M. "When the Blues Get You Down." *Better Homes and Gardens* (July 1974), 52:12,16-18.

"Mental State of the Union." *Newsweek* (Oct. 15, 1984), 104:113.

Nicholi, Armand Mayo II. "Why Can't I Deal with Depression?" *Christianity Today* (Nov. 11, 1983), 27:38-41.

"Polling for Mental Health." *Time* (Oct. 15, 1984), 124:80.

"Sad Moms/Sad Babies." *Psychology Today* (Dec. 1983), 17:14.

Shaver, Phillip. "Down at College." *Psychology Today* (May 1983), 17:16.

Smith, Dinitia. "The New Puritans: Deprivation Chic." *New York* (June 11, 1984), 24-29.

PAMPHLETS

Corfman, Eunice. "Depression, Manic-Depressive Illness, and Biological Rhythms." Rockville, MD: National Institute of Mental Health, 1982.

"Depression: Dark Night of the Soul." Mental Health Association, Department of Health Information Services. West Point, PA: Merck, Sharp and Donohue.

Depression Skills: Getting Down, Getting Up! Weymouth, MA: Life Skills Education, Inc., n.d.

"Depression: What You Should Do About It." Arlington, VA: National Mental Health Association, 1981.

"Facts About Mental Health." Arlington, VA: Mental Health Association, 1979.

"How to Deal with Your Tensions." Mental Health Association, 1981.

Irwin, Theodore. "Depression: Causes and Treatment." Public Affairs Pamphlet No. 488. New York: Public Affairs Committee, 1980.

"Medicine for the Layman, Depression and Manic-Depressive Illness." Bethesda, MD: National Institute of Health, U.S. Department of Health and Human Services, Feb. 1982.